KU-661-000

VAN GOGH'S EAR

Best World Poetry & Prose

Volume 4

Ian Ayres, Editor

COMMITTEE ON POETRY • NEW YORK
FRENCH CONNECTION PRESS • PARIS

FOUNDER & EDITOR:
Ian Ayres

DESIGN & LAYOUT: Ian Ayres
PROOFREADING & RESEARCH: Eric Elléna, Dean Doser
PUBLIC RELATIONS & EVENTS: Avishay Artsy, Mark Lipman
SALES: Peter Hale, Mark Lipman • COMPUTER GURU: Antoine Loakira
ADMINISTRATION: Eric Elléna, Peter Hale, Bob Rosenthal
ACCOUNTING: Kay Spurlock, Sandrine Surget

Many thanks to the whole team!

Cover digital artwork © 2004 Mohammad Shamsul Arefin, Cyberjaya

Van Gogh's Ear *is a joint publication of*
Committee on Poetry (New York) and French Connection Press (Paris)

COMMITTEE ON POETRY
P. O. Box 582, Stuyvesant Station, New York, NY 10009 U.S.A.

GALWAY COUNTY LIBRARIES

2161.617
£15.00

821
COL

french CONNECTION press

FRENCH CONNECTION PRESS
12 rue Lamartine, 75009 Paris France • www.frenchcx.com

Copyright © 2005 by French Connection Press / Committee on Poetry
All rights revert to authors upon publication.

All rights reserved. Except for brief passages quoted in newspaper,
magazine, radio, or television reviews, no part of this book may be
reproduced in any form or by any means, electronic or mechanical,
including photocopying or recording, or by information storage or
retrieval system, without permission in writing from the Publisher.

Printed in Canada
ISBN 2-914853-03-3

"If everyone demanded peace instead of another television set, then there'd be peace."

—John Lennon
1940-1980

"Gardez cet objet précieusement."

—Vincent van Gogh
December 23, 1888

Vincent cuts off his ear on a Sunday evening, two days before Christmas. At 11:30 p.m., he arrives at brothel number 1, asks for Rachel, and hands her his ear, saying, "Keep this object carefully." He then disappears. The police find him at home the next day, lying in bed, apparently lifeless.

BEST LETTER | TO THE EDITOR

Editor's Note: The following is in response to a letter from Carolyn Cassady that appears in Volume 3 of *Van Gogh's Ear*. We'd be more than interested in your response, dear reader, to this letter from Fay Zwicky. The best response will be included in the next *Van Gogh's Ear*, which will be Volume 5 of our anthology series.

11 February 2004

Dear Ian,

Thank you very much for sending *Van Gogh's Ear 2004* – a remarkably varied and often intriguing collection faithfully reflecting your expressed eclecticism. Sorry that so many of your contributors are dead (or almost – I'm 71), I particularly warmed to the poems of James Kirkup, Lawrence Ferlinghetti, Guy Kettelhack, Felice Picano and Denise Levertov. In fact, Levertov's poignant 'A Hundred A Day' extends, deepens and sheds further light on Carolyn Cassady's decision to remain *hors de combat*.

Informed by more than a whiff of battle fatigue, Cassady's cultural lament has a familiar ring. New England's high-minded Transcendentalists armed with moral and aesthetic responsibility to the exigencies of their craft, their duty to bear witness haunt the plaint of her disappointed idealism. Her remark that "there is little of higher insights into our human condition to help us rise on our upward spiral journey of evolution" is pure Emerson. He, too, argued that music is as necessary to poetry as language, following Plato's proposition that poetry's rhythms and harmonies "sink furthest into the depths of the soul and take hold of it most firmly by bringing it nobility and grace." The obligation to communicate with readers was understood, the contract honoured on both sides.

Those of us born before World War II who set off with similar ideals, tucked behind our fences of meter and ambiguous irony, paying our ancestral dues, are now uncomfortably aware that what mattered to us has become irrelevant to succeeding generations, that we're losing whatever it was we set out to achieve. It doesn't mean, however, that we should throw in the towel and hand over the keys of the city to the barbarians.

Unafraid to invoke Matthew Arnold's ghost, Denise Levertov knew what was being lost in a society dominated by mass-communications and consumerism, grasped the cultural shift from printed word to visual image, knew impending disaster in her bones. But out of this knowledge came her wonderful poem. It doesn't delude itself, knows the precariousness of life and its imperfections but registers that fragility with the force of life-giving epiphany. Once you're more in touch with human vulnerability, especially your own, you become less concerned to censure and condemn the ignorant armies and more to nurture the values in which you continue to have faith, however wavering. You may even come to recognize writing as an aspect of wise living and poems not as summit or vanguard but as part of some larger more humbling tale.

I, too, have feelings that I live in a culture in which I don't seem to have a legitimate place. Much of what I cared for seems to have been forgotten or remains unread. Much of what is touted as poetry is both obscure and unintelligible. Yet, old-fashioned or not, read or unread, it's necessary to survival that I keep writing, remembering, and refusing to give up. That's why I sent you a poem [for *Van Gogh's Ear 3*] and, to my surprise and delight, you accepted it. I wish Carolyn Cassady had done the same.

With best wishes and thanks,

Sincerely,

Fay Zwicky

Contents

Poetry & Prose

Illustrations

A BRAVE AND STARTLING TRUTH

Dedicated to the hope for peace, which lies, sometimes hidden, in every heart.

We, the people, on a small and lonely planet
Traveling through casual space
Past aloof stars, across the way of indifferent suns
To a destination where all signs tell us
It is possible and imperative that we learn
A brave and startling truth.

And when we come to it
To the day of peacemaking
When we release our fingers
From fists of hostility
And allow the pure air to cool our palms

When we come to it
When the curtain falls on the minstrel show of hate
And face sooted with scorn are scrubbed clean
When battlefields and coliseum
No longer rake our unique and particular sons and
        daughters
Up with bruised and bloody grass
To lie in identical plots in foreign soil

When the rapacious storming of the churches
The screaming racket in the temples have ceased
When the pennants are waving gaily
When the banners of the world tremble
Stoutly in the good, clean breeze

When we come to it
When we let the rifles fall from our shoulders
And children dress their dolls in flags of truce
When land mines of death have been removed
And the aged can walk into evenings of peace
When religious ritual is not perfumed
By the incense of burning flesh
And childhood dreams are not kicked awake
By nightmares of abuse

When we come to it
Then we will confess that not the Pyramids
With their stones set in mysterious perfection
Nor the Gardens of Babylon
Hanging as eternal beauty
In our collective memory
Not the Grand Canyon
Kindled into delicious color
By Western sunsets

Nor the Danube, flowing its blue soul into Europe
Not the sacred peak of Mount Fuji
Stretching to the Rising Sun
Neither Father Amazon nor Mother Mississippi
    who, without favor,
Nurtures all creatures in the depths and on the shores
These are not the only wonders of the world

When we come to it
We, this people, on this minuscule and kithless globe
Who reach daily for the bomb, the blade and the
    dagger
Yet who petition in the dark for tokens of peace

We, this people, on this mote of matter
In whose mouths abide cankerous words
Which challenge our very existence
Yet out of those same mouths
Come songs of such exquisite sweetness
That the heart falters in its labor
And the body is quieted into awe

We, this people, on this small and drifting planet
Whose hands can strike with such abandon
That, in a twinkling, life is sapped from the living
Yet those same hands can touch with such healing,
    irresistible tenderness,
That the haughty neck is happy to bow
And the proud back is glad to bend
Out of such chaos, of such contradiction
We learn that we are neither devils nor divines

When we come to it
We, this people, on this wayward, floating body
Created on this earth, of this earth
Have the power to fashion for this earth
A climate where every man and every woman
Can live freely without sanctimonious piety
Without crippling fear

When we come to it
We must confess that we are the possible
We are the miraculous, the true wonder of this world
That is when, and only when
We come to it.

Margaret Atwood

ON WRITING POETRY

Waterstone's Poetry Lecture. Delivered at Hay On Wye, Wales, June 1995.

I'm supposed to be talking in a vaguely autobiographical way about the connection between life and poetry, or at least between my life and my poetry. I recently read an account of a study which intends to show how writers of a certain age—my age, roughly—attempt to "seize control" of the stories of their own lives by deviously concocting their own biographies. However, it's a feature of our age that if you write a work of fiction, everyone assumes that the people and events in it are disguised biography—but if you write your biography, it's equally assumed you're lying your head off.

This last may be true, at any rate of poets: Plato said that poets should be excluded from the ideal republic because they are such liars. I am a poet, and I affirm that this is true. About no subject are poets tempted to lie so much as about their own lives; I know one of them who has floated at least five versions of his autobiography, none of them true. I of course—being also a novelist—am a much more truthful person than that. But since poets lie, how can you believe me?

Here then is the official version of my life as a poet:

I was once a snub-nosed blonde. My name was Betty. I had a perky personality and was a cheerleader for the college football team. My favourite colour was pink. Then I became a poet. My hair darkened overnight, my nose lengthened, I gave up football for the cello, my real name disappeared and was replaced by one that had a chance of being taken seriously by the literati, and my clothes changed colour in the closet, all by themselves, from pink to black. I stopped humming the songs from *Oklahoma* and began quoting Kierkegaard. And not only that—all of my high heeled shoes lost their heels, and were magically transformed into sandals. Needless to say, my many boyfriends took one look at this and ran screaming from the scene as if their toenails were on fire. New ones replaced them; they all had beards.

Believe it or not, there is an element of truth in this story. It's the bit about the name, which was not Betty but something equally non-poetic, and with the same number of letters. It's also the bit about the boyfriends. But meanwhile, here is the real truth:

I became a poet at the age of sixteen. I did not intend to do it. It was not my fault.

Allow me to set the scene for you. The year was 1956. Elvis Presley had just appeared on the Ed Sullivan Show, from the waist up. At school dances, which were held in the gymnasium and smelled like armpits, the dance with the most charisma was rock'n'roll. The approved shoes were saddle shoes and white bucks, the evening gowns were strapless, if you could manage it; they had crinolined skirts that made you look like half a cabbage with a little radish head. Girls were forbidden to wear jeans to school, except on football days, when they sat on the hill to watch, and it was feared that the boys would be able to see up their dresses unless they wore pants. TV dinners had just been invented.

None of this—you might think, and rightly—was conducive to the production of poetry. If someone had told me a year previously that I would suddenly turn into a poet, I would have giggled. Yet this is what did happen.

I was in my fourth year of high school. The high school was in Toronto, which in the year 1956 was still known as Toronto the Good because of its puritanical liquor laws. It had a population of six hundred and fifty thousand, five hundred and nine people at the time, and was a synonym for bland propriety. The high school I attended was also a synonym for bland propriety, and although it has produced a steady stream of chartered accountants and one cabinet minister, no other poets have ever emerged from it, before or since.

The day I became a poet was a sunny day of no particular ominousness. I was walking across the football field, not because I was sports-minded or had plans to smoke a cigarette behind the field house—the only other reason for going there—but because this was my normal way home from school. I was scuttling along in my usual furtive way, suspecting no ill, when a large invisible thumb descended from the sky and pressed down on the top of my head. A poem formed. It was quite a gloomy poem: the poems of the young usually are. It was a gift, this poem—a gift from an anonymous donor, and, as such, both exciting and sinister at the same time.

I suspect this is the way all poets begin writing poetry, only they don't want to admit it, so they make up more rational explanations. But this is the true explanation, and I defy anyone to disprove it.

The poem that I composed on that eventful day, although entirely without merit or even promise, did have some features. It rhymed and scanned, because we had been taught rhyming and scansion at school. It resembled the poetry of Lord Byron and Edgar Allan Poe, with a little Shelley and Keats thrown in. The fact is that at the time I became a poet, I had read very few poems written after the year 1900. I knew nothing of modernism or free verse. These were not the only things I knew nothing of. I had no idea, for instance, that I was about to step into a whole set of preconceptions and social roles which had to do with what poets were like, how they should behave, and what they ought to wear; moreover, I did not know that the rules about these things were different if you were female. I did not know that "poetess" was an insult, and that I myself would some day be called one. I did not know that to be told I had transcended my gender would be considered a compliment. I didn't know—yet—that black was compulsory. All of that was in the future. When I was sixteen, it was simple. Poetry existed; therefore it could be written; and nobody had told me—yet—the many, many reasons why it could not be written by me.

At first glance, there was little in my background to account for the descent of the large thumb of poetry onto the top of my head. But let me try to account for my own poetic genesis.

I was born on November 18, 1939, in the Ottawa General Hospital, two and a half months after the beginning of the Second World War. Being born at the beginning of the war gave me a substratum of anxiety and dread to draw on, which is very useful to a poet. It also meant that I was malnourished. This is why I am short. If it hadn't been for food rationing, I would have been six feet tall.

I saw my first balloon in 1946, one that had been saved from before the war. It was inflated for me as a treat when I had the mumps on my sixth birthday, and it broke immediately. This was a major influence on my later work.

As for my birth month, a detail of much interest to poets, obsessed as they are with symbolic systems of all kinds: I was not pleased, during my childhood, to have been born in November, as there wasn't much inspiration for birthday party motifs. February children got hearts, May ones flowers, but what was there for me? A cake surrounded by withered leaves? November was a drab, dark and wet month, lacking even snow; its only noteworthy festival was Remembrance Day. But in adult life I discovered that November was, astrologically speaking, the month of sex, death and regeneration, and that November First was the Day of the Dead. It still wouldn't have been much good for birthday parties, but it was just fine for poetry, which tends to revolve a good deal around sex and death, with regeneration optional.

Six months after I was born, I was taken by packsack to a remote cabin in north-western Quebec, where my father was doing research as a forest entomologist. I should add here that my parents were unusual for their time. Both of them liked being as far away from civilization as possible, my mother because she hated housework and tea parties, my father because he liked chopping wood. They also weren't much interested in what the sociologists would call rigid sex-role stereotyping. This was a help to me in later life, and helped me to get a job at summer camp teaching small boys to start fires.

My childhood was divided between the forest, in the warmer parts of the year, and various cities, in the colder parts. I was thus able to develop the rudiments of the double personality so necessary for a poet. I also had lots of time for meditation. In the bush there were no theatres, movies, parades, or very functional radios; there were also not many other people. The result was that I learned to read early—I was lucky enough to have a mother who read out loud, but she couldn't be doing it all the time and you had to amuse yourself with something or other when it rained. I became a reading addict, and have remained so ever since. "You'll ruin your eyes," I was told when caught at my secret vice under the covers with a flashlight. I did so, and would do it again. Like cigarette addicts who will smoke mattress stuffing if all else fails, I will read anything. As a child I read a good many things I shouldn't have, but this also is useful for poetry.

As the critic Norththrop Frye has said, we learn poetry through the seat of our pants, by being bounced up and down to nursery rhymes as children. Poetry is essentially oral, and is close to song; rhythm precedes meaning. My first experiences with poetry were Mother Goose, which contains some of the most surrealistic poems in the English language, and whatever singing commercials could be picked up on the radio, such as:

> You'll wonder where the yellow went
> When you brush your teeth with Pepsodent!

I created my first book of poetry at the age of five. To begin with, I made the book itself, cutting the pages out of scribbler paper and sewing them together in what I did not know was the traditional signature fashion. Then I copied into the book all the poems I could remember, and when there were some blank pages left at the end, I added a few of my own to complete it. This book was an entirely satisfying art object for me; so satisfying that I felt I had nothing more to say in that direction, and gave up writing poetry altogether for another eleven years.

My English teacher from 1955, run to ground by some documentary crew trying to explain my life, said that in her class I had showed no particular promise. This was true. Until the descent of the giant thumb, I showed no particular promise. I also showed no particular promise for some time afterwards, but I did not know this. A lot of being a poet consists of willed ignorance. If you woke up from your trance and realized the nature of the life-threatening and dignity-destroying precipice you were walking along, you would switch into actuarial sciences immediately.

2161.617

If I had not been ignorant in this particular way, I would not have announced to an assortment of my high school female friends, in the cafeteria one brown-bag lunchtime, that I was going to be a writer. I said "writer," not "poet;" I did have some common sense. But my announcement was certainly a conversation-stopper. Sticks of celery were suspended in mid-crunch, peanut-butter sandwiches paused halfway between table and mouth; nobody said a word. One of those present reminded me of this incident recently—I had repressed it—and said she had been simply astounded. "Why?" I said. "Because I wanted to be a writer?" "No," she said. "Because you had the guts to say it out loud."

GALWAY COUNTY LIBRARIES

But I was not conscious of having guts, or even of needing them. We obsessed folks, in our youth, are oblivious to the effects of our obsessions; only later do we develop enough cunning to conceal them, or at least to avoid mentioning them at cocktail parties. The one good thing to be said about announcing yourself as a writer in the colonial Canadian fifties is that nobody told me I couldn't do it because I was a girl. They simply found the entire proposition ridiculous. Writers were dead and English, or else extremely elderly and American; they were not sixteen years old and Canadian. It would have been worse if I'd been a boy, though. Never mind the fact that all the really stirring poems I'd read at that time had been about slaughter, mayhem, sex and death—poetry was thought of as existing in the pastel female realm, along with embroidery and flower arranging. If I'd been male I would probably have had to roll around in the mud, in some boring skirmish over whether or not I was a sissy.

I'll skip over the embarrassingly bad poems I published in the high school year book—had I no shame?—well, actually, no—mentioning only briefly the word of encouragement I received from my wonderful Grade 12 English teacher, Miss Bessie Billings—"I can't understand a word of this, dear, so it must be good." I will not go into the dismay of my parents, who worried—with good reason—over how I would support myself. I will pass over my flirtation with journalism as a way of making a living, an idea I dropped when I discovered that in the fifties—unlike now—female journalists always ended up writing the obituaries and the ladies' page.

But how was I to make a living? There was not a roaring market in poetry, there, then. I thought of running away and being a waitress, which I later tried, but got very tired and thin; there's nothing like clearing away other people's mushed-up dinners to make you lose your appetite. Finally I went into English Literature at university, having decided in a cynical manner that I could always teach to support my writing habit. Once I got past the Anglo-Saxon it was fun, although I did suffer a simulated cardiac arrest the first time I encountered T.S. Eliot and realized that not all poems rhymed, any more. "I don't understand a word of this," I thought, "so it must be good."

After a year or two of keeping my head down and trying to pass myself off as a normal person, I made contact with the five other people at my university who were interested in writing; and through them, and some of my teachers, I discovered that there was a whole subterranean Wonderland of Canadian writing that was going on just out of general earshot and sight. It was not large—in 1960 you were doing well to sell 200 copies of a book of poems by a Canadian, and a thousand novels was a best-seller; there were only five literary magazines, which ran on the life blood of their editors; but it was very integrated. Once in—that is, once published in a magazine—it was as if you'd been given a Masonic handshake or a key to the underground railroad. All of a sudden you were part of a conspiracy.

People sometimes ask me about my influences; these were, by and large, the Canadian poets of my own generation and that just before mine. P.K. Page, Margaret Avison, Jay Macpherson, James Reaney, Irving Layton, Leonard Cohen, Al Purdy, D.G. Jones, Eli Mandel, John Newlove, Gwendolyn MacEwen, Michael Ondaatje, Pat Lane, George Bowering, Milton Acorn, A.M. Klein, Alden Nowlan, Elizabeth Brewster, Anne Wilkinson—these are some of the poets who were writing and publishing then, whom I knew, and whose poetry I read. People writing about Canadian poetry at that time spoke a lot about the necessity of creating a Canadian literature. There was a good deal of excitement, and the feeling that you were in on the ground floor, so to speak.

So poetry was a vital form, and it quickly acquired a public dimension. Above ground the bourgeoisie reined supreme, in their two-piece suits and ties and camel-hair coats and pearl earrings (not all of this worn by the same sex); but at night the Bohemian world came alive, in various nooks and crannies of Toronto, sporting black turtlenecks, drinking coffee at little tables with red-checked tablecloths and candles stuck in Chianti bottles, in coffee houses,—well—in the one coffee house in town—listening to jazz and folk singing, reading their poems out loud as if they'd never heard it was stupid, and putting swear words into them. For a twenty-year-old this was intoxicating stuff.

By this time I had my black wardrobe more or less together, and had learned not to say, "Well, hi there!" in sprightly tones. I was publishing in little magazines, and shortly thereafter I started to write reviews for them too. I didn't know what I was talking about, but I soon began to find out. Every year for four years, I put together a collection of my poems and submitted it to a publishing house; every year it was—to my dismay then, to my relief now—rejected. Why was I so eager to be published right away? Like all twenty-one-year-old poets, I thought I would be dead by thirty, and Sylvia Plath had not set a helpful example. For a while there, you were made to feel that, if a poet and female, you could not really be serious about it unless you'd made at least one suicide attempt. So I felt I was running out of time.

My poems were still not very good, but by now they showed—how shall I put it?—a sort of twisted and febrile glimmer. In my graduating year, a group of them won the main poetry prize at the University. Madness took hold of me, and with the aid of a friend, and another friend's flatbed press, we printed them. A lot of poets published their own work then; unlike novels, poetry was short, and therefore cheap to do. We had to print each poem separately, and then disassemble it, as there were not enough a's for the whole book; the cover was done with a lino-block. We printed 250 copies, and sold them through bookstores, for 50 cents each. They now go in the rare book trade for eighteen hundred dollars a pop. Wish I'd kept some.

Three years or so later—after two years at graduate school at the dreaded Harvard University, two broken engagements, a year of living in a tiny rooming-house room and working at a market research company which was more fun than a barrel of drugged monkeys and a tin of orange-flavoured rice pudding—and after the massive rejection of my first novel, and of several other poetry collections as well— and not to mention my first confusing trip to Europe, I ended up in British Columbia, teaching grammar to Engineering students at eight-thirty in the morning in a Quonset hut. It was all right, as none of us were awake; I made them write imitations of Kafka, which I thought might help them in their chosen profession.

In comparison with the few years I had just gone through, this was sort of like going to heaven. I lived in an apartment built on top of somebody's house, and had scant furniture; but not only did I have a 180 degree view of Vancouver harbour, but I also had all night to write in. I taught in the daytime, ate canned food, did not wash my dishes until all of them were dirty—the biologist in me became very interested in the different varieties of moulds that could be grown on leftover Kraft dinner—and stayed up until four in the morning. I completed, in that one year, my first officially-published book of poems and my first published novel, which I wrote on blank exam booklets, as well as a number of short stories and the beginnings of two other novels, later completed. It was an astonishingly productive year for me. I looked like the Night of the Living Dead. Art has its price.

This first book of poems was called *The Circle Game*; I designed the cover myself, using stick-on dots—we were very cost-effective in those days—and to everyone's surprise, especially mine, it won a prize called The Governor General's Award, which in Canada was the big one to win. Literary prizes are a crapshoot, and I was lucky that year. I was back at Harvard by then, mopping up the uncompleted work for my doctorate—I never did finish it—and living with three roommates, whose names were Judy and Sue and Karen. To collect the prize I had to attend a ceremony in Ottawa, at Government House, which meant dressups—and it was obvious to all of us, as we went through the two items in my wardrobe, that I had nothing to wear. Sue leant me the dress and earrings, Judy the shoes, and while I was away they incinerated my clunky rubber-soled Hush Puppy shoes, having decided that these did not go with my new, poetic image.

This was an act of treachery, but they were right. I was now a recognised poet, and had a thing or two to live up to. It took me a while to get the hair right, but I have finally settled down with a sort of modified Celtic look, which is about the only thing available to me short of baldness. I no longer feel I'll be dead by thirty; now it's sixty. I suppose these deadlines we set for ourselves are really a way of saying we appreciate time, and want to use all of it. I'm still writing, I'm still writing poetry, I still can't explain why, and I'm still running out of time.

Wordsworth was sort of right when he said, "Poets in their youth begin in gladness / But thereof comes in the end despondency and madness." Except that sometimes poets skip the gladness and go straight to the despondency. Why is that? Part of it is the conditions under which poets work—giving all, receiving little in return from an age that by and large ignores them—and part of it is cultural expectation—"The lunatic, the lover and the poet," says Shakespeare, and notice which comes first. My own theory is that poetry is composed with the melancholy side of the brain, and that if you do nothing but, you may find yourself going slowly down a long dark tunnel with no exit. I have avoided this by being ambidextrous: I write novels too. But when I find myself writing poetry again, it always has the surprise of that first unexpected and anonymous gift.

AFTER NIETZSCHE

Brown velvet couch, standing vacuum tube radio, brass bed.

She walked down the hall naming and touching each object. It seemed to ease them better into their places, calm them, quiet the house.

Gas stove, heavy old typewriter, armoire.

A feeling permeated the house. It was not deforestation or disenfranchisement. It was the heart having been ripped out at the roots. She felt it and so did the objects around her, down to the Model T out back, the empty can of soup, her grandmother's silver butter dish.

Sadness was not a general blanket pain, as it had been before, it was repetitive stupidity over small insignificances when she was too tired to fight any longer. Loneliness was a smell. She missed a curve of belly flesh and the corner of 8th Avenue and 2nd Street. Anger – being belittled for who she was, equally for not being seen at all.

Down comforter, Oxford English Dictionary with magnifying glass.

She was listening, by this point to all the objects in the house, exhausted to the point of euphoria, touching and calming each in its particular way. Following their patterns.

It was the smaller things that were harder to separate and keep track of.

Children's underwear. One purple sock. Stuffed Dalmatian, rotary phone, potted thyme.

As objects got smaller they became strident, each object in danger of coming unglued. As a child her mother taught her, each object has a place, each object in its place.

Marbles, Chinese jump rope, dreidel.

These were in the drawer, but she forgot where the most important things had gone. Worse, she had no idea how to get them back. Only how to work what was in the house with her at any given moment. It varied so.

She watched the catalpa stitched curtain blow in and out the window at night and with it the sense of who or what was missing. The feelings being so too. Rage at massacres of herself and others. Humiliation being a parade naked and crying down the street ending in front of a room of laughing people. She could touch these. Not emptiness. Emptiness had noting to touch.

Wash cloth, hair ribbon, baby shampoo.

FIRST FEMALE ASTRONAUT

Earth

solid, earth
  dense, earth full, earth
    round, earth masses
      out presses
        in dips
          down mounds
            up soft
              rain falls silent
                mist rises hiss
of breeze sways
  sweet scent of wheat of grass of green
    growing over massed
      mountains over dipped
        valleys sends crisp
          colors into leaves, fruit
            bulges then
              heavy snow hushed
                on mountaintop, valley
deep then buds
  swell forth breast
    of earth heaves soft
      hiss of breeze sways
        sweet scent of green
          growing.

Wendy

walks forth on girdled
  asphalt streets on fist
    of concrete closed
      tight, under needling
        skyscrapers past ripping
          jackhammers whizzing
            cars Wendy walks with solid
              feet heavy-shod, soft
                curves shrouded, smile

flung out like a protective arm fending off
    faceless passersby who trod and plod, Wendy
        rushes through lecture halls where science
            probes history
                dissects philosophy
                    rips questions
                        bulldoze her heart, answers
                            leave it stripmined Wendy whizzes
to airport
    hustle-bustle
        through airport
            hurley-burley high
                above the Atlantic, Wendy watches
                    from behind thickpaned windows as waves
                        plead like upturned faces, straining
                            for shore like babies
                              for the breast, sadness
swells Wendy's heart, flows
    forth to mix with
        jetplane exhaust spuming out over
            sea's hungry mouth until,
                exhausted, she leans
                    her head against the glass, whispers, "This
                      is too much I can't take this
                        anymore," falls
                          into troubled sleep.
Wendy dreams of a great she-bear curled
    in her cave while snow hushes
        mountaintop, valley
            deep inside her brain fingers
                of memory close
                    like a fist: last season's
                    litter the season
                      before that the season
                        before that, faceless cubs
probe her fur with needling
    claws tug
        her dugs with hungry

                    mouths then waking, she
                        rises, shakes
                            shaggy fur, lumbers
                                out to sniff first scent of green
                                    growing but earth
                                        is gone all
is black like a cave's
    vaulted roof, paws
        turn into gloved
            hands and booted
                feet, snout
                    turns into helmet, fur
                        crinkles into a metallic
                            suit, the lone astronaut drifts
                                through space, lifeline
dangling like a severed
    umbilical cord, inside her brain a fist
        opens from behind
            thickpaned visor she whispers,

                                                "I remember
heat like an icy shroud

                                                I remember
highways snapping like garters

                                                I remember
skyscrapers buckling like crumpled clothes

                                                I remember
flesh flashing into photo
negatives, skeletons akimbo like crazed
X-Rays, shadows seared
into sidewalks

                                                I remember
tidal waves and quakes, earth's
womb giving one final cramped

heave then fire like blood
gushing then
ash falling a hush
like snow then a merciless
sun a violent
wind a swirl
of sand whirl
of continents into one
vast desert then dust
trailing into the sky."

                                                    Wendy
        whimpers in sleep, pressed
            into airplane seat she curls
                her arms around herself feels
                    flesh dense and
                        solid, full and
                            round, still
                                dreaming she whispers,
                                    "Mommy, I'm sorry, Mommy,
        I won't do it again, Mommy
            forgive me, Mommy,
                love me again." Tears fall
                    soft as rain, she wakes, rises: plane
                        has dipped down on runway, passengers
                            smile, mound
                                out through open
                                    door sending crisp
                                        footsteps down hallways,
        sidewalks into whizzing
            cars, Wendy's smile swells, buds, breast
                heaving she breathes
                    deeply, sighs
                        a sweet scent of green
                            growing, walks forth onto

                                                    Earth.

Découpe Fraîche. Painting by Barbara Philipp (www.barbaraphilipp.com)
Oil on Canvas, Paris, France 2002

Courtesy Barbara Philipp Collection

Ian Ayres

KITCHEN NOTE TO THE MASSES

Whether you're a cuntlicker or a cocksucker
you are human you are human you are human
meat with a mouth for meat tho taste buds vary
very very rump to the door that won't stay shut
like your mother's thighs the moment you were
began with meat thrusting meat your parents only
2 people who fucked & you born to suck nipple
till carnivorous teething bit her breast such suckage
   leaving you to lick your plate & eyeball the cook
   (some French hummer you'd gobble *soixante-neuf*)
Kant seems to have treated all sex this way, holding that
"sexual love makes of the loved person an object of appetite;
as soon as that appetite has been stilled, the person is cast aside
as one casts away a lemon which has been sucked dry"
   & i wanna lick *you* from head to toe
   noshing a daisy chain blown by the bisexual by
   gusts of tonsil hockey in meatless catacombs
   your head awhirl with skull-fuck
     "you look good enough to eat," mouths James Dean
      hungering for Elizabeth Taylor on celluloid
the lip service you desire in a field of fingerprints
where hanging orgasms drip spasms thru
     at throat strained stranglings
     strangers all in one skin
on sale against pissed-on walls Xperienced enough to know
assholes can be fun in bed
     fuckfuckfuckfuckfuck
     unspaced
tongue sandwiches are in the fridge & the rest is
   Shakespeare or silence or something like that

Ian Ayres

EFFLUX FOR DOUGLAS OLIVER

you were this man in a bed this man dying man dying and it seemed
you'd go on dying for a lifetime and it just took some getting used to
but I never thought you'd actually die though you glimpsed a deer
waiting to take you home on its back you glimpsed a deer no you
couldn't die because you were a friend to me and I cared about you
and how can anyone I care about die? you left me yet when you did
yeah I know you left others too you left others who were
                                        much closer to you
but I am selfish and disturbed I laugh remembering what you said the
last time when it was about Time that you spoke of wanting to write
two more books before you go you told me you couldn't help me
untwist my twisted morals but would help with my writing if only on
occasion because Now is precious Time and Time is running out—you
had three weeks left exactly three weeks to the two-thousandth not so
good Good Friday when at about nine-thirty post meridiem you shed
your Douglas Oliver skin. did you rise out of your body and witness
all of your suffering rise up in your loved-ones helplessly watching
tears drop down from their beautiful eyes? did the hospital ceiling
open up into a tunnel of light where the deer awaited you? will your
little son be on the deer with you for the funeral the flames the
scattering of your ashes in Paris? there are so many
                                        questions I want to ask
so many questions I wanted to ask you Doug but your generous
knowledge mesmerized me each time we met and I'd forget I'd
forget to ask what cancer felt like the pain the pain I saw on your
face the pain that morphine could only put spaces between the pain
what was the pain? had it the bite of tooth decay except the nerves
being eaten away all over the body? no it was your lower back back
back in August wasn't it? when did it start I forget I forget but I
won't forget you because you took the time to guide me in my
writing when you had so little time left you cared you actually cared
and that touched my heart Doug. you told me that all your friends are
kind of kooky not in those words but that was your point and you made
the point that I too was of

your kooky friends

and that was the moment that was the moment that some find
embarrassing to mention that was the moment when you expressed
what makes this life worth living if only you were living now but I
know you're standing here next to me as I get this out though I've
got to admit I had no intention of letting your death get to me I'd
made up my mind that day near the end when you asked me to cut
down on my visits it felt like rejection like I had to block out the
knowing that I'd never again hear you speak and speak man you
could speak and the words you'd speak fascinated me yeah I wanted
to spend as much time as I could with you because of because and
that leads right into the gold of your mind you'd share so freely
though you were in pain and making an effort to stay clear on

foggy morphine

now I don't know if I'm imagining this or not but I feel your
presence your hand on my shoulder and I know you're still with us
oh yes Doug I remember I remember when I asked you if you were
scared and you said not really but tears came into your eyes when you
told me the hardest part the real pain worse than the lower back
worse than anything at all was having to leave the people you love
it's the parting it's the finality the no hope of at least postcard
communication—send a postcard Doug wherever you are from
wherever you are send a picture postcard of you on the deer with
your little son telling us it's okay you're okay we'll all be okay

21 April 2000

Ian Ayres

IF TREES COULD RUN

Silent timbre in the notwithstanding. Notwithstanding. Still. One losing a limb it must switch back to. Climb the limit lost. Up the winding breakage as compared with. Winding wind and where and would. Where would they run to. Notwithstanding. Still in the frequent loss. Where uprooted could they scoot to. At or in what whether. Permitting either and and both. Or in drought of fire flooding. Where as ashes could they float to. Where on soil could they hide. From the ax withal sapped gradual. In as to knotted be not. Through tough and fibrous disentangled. Swiftly hence to groundless whither. On abouts event so turning. Leaves clearing stride. So ever into by fore worming. Out where coffins no more would. Cut to burn. Notwithstanding. Still. To be running. If running could.

BETWEEN THE WILD AND CIVILIZATION

Sky's suitcase knocked a small hole
in the window when he moved in—
small, but not too small for a smart baboon
to punch it larger, reach around, open the door
and invite the troop in,
right after Sky went off to celebrate
his first manager's job at a bush camp in Botswana.

The baboons defecated on his bed,
yanked down the drapes, ripped up
his clothes, smashed his camera, destroyed
his computer, drank the shampoo, ate the food
and left.

Every troop has a head mischief-maker.
Sky tracked him down, spray-painted him white and
let him go. When the troop saw the white baboon
running toward them, they got scared, ran away,
and when he chased after them, they ran some more
until all the baboons had left the area. Sky's friends
thought it was a good joke.

In the end, the troop turned on the white baboon and killed him.

What else did Sky expect?

REUNION

Harris, Vermont. IBM moves away,
Ford plant closes, Harris Machine & Tool
lays off 80. "I dodged the bullet,"
Jessie's dad tells him when he calls.
Two months later, HM&T declares bankruptcy,
doesn't tell its workers—and Tuesday, this week,
they fire Jessie's dad—no severance.
Friday, Jessie drives up with six bags
of food, spends the weekend
cooking with his dad.
Sunday evening, Jessie says,
"I'll keep an eye out, Dad."
"Don't worry about me, Jessie. I'm 5th generation
in this town—not leaving just because you did."
Turning onto Main Street, Jessie parks in back of
Duffy's Tavern, *Where the Elite Meet to Eat.*
The *One For The Road* sign's still behind the bar
with the neon Superman flying over it, holding up
a mug of coffee. Jessie orders the café du jour—
Hawaiian Macadamia—watches the Knicks
lose another game, leaves the bartender
a couple extra bucks. Then, about to
get back in his car, he feels a knife
against his ribs. A voice says,
"I'll take the keys."
Jessie whips around, the knife
gashes his jacket. "Dennis!"
They went to high school together,
got stoned on pot brownies in 9th grade, played
in a band together junior year—

"You outta your fuckin' mind, Dennis!
You're gonna steal my car?!"
"Leave me alone, Jessie. I'm all messed up."
"So, what else is new?"
Dennis laughs. "I thought you were from outta town."

Amanda Bay

CALIFORNIA SONG

Open the blinds to the ocean, make gourmet coffee in a shapely Italian pot. Enter the day as the sun burns through the fog.

An old friend from Berkeley tells you, with no irony, that she's worried the neighbors' child has more toys than her own.

Put your sorrow in your pocket, walk along the beach. Listen to Wilco and shiver. You could walk forever, feet in sand, head in sky, with this American sound.

The waves roll and break, endlessly, endlessly, endless . . . .

In town, see how oddly money merges with a clamour for health and transcendence. Yoga studios and natural hair dyes charm and seduce. The people in Whole Foods dress exquisitely in sweatsuits.

At sunset an orange globe slips behind purple, wispy streaks, all poised to plummet into the sea. Your exhaustion is uncanny.

Evening news gives out the image of another continent: a bony, expressionless baby, cradled in a desperate mother's arms. It seems they are a bad investment.

Float toward unconsciousness, the waves rolling and breaking, endlessly, endlessly, endless . . . . Watery percussions.
Listen to the words:
> Relax your hands around what they hold;
>> Relax your hands around what they hold.

David Bergman

FROM THE ARCHIVES OF RECOVERED MEMORY

*"There's a station in my memory. We have to go through a barrier,
papers are shown and looked at—maybe false ones."*

—Binjamin Wilkomirski

Now that we have come to the edge of sleep,
we can allow ourselves to remember what never happened,
permit the exposure of crimes concealed
just behind the bland ordinariness of our small routines.

For this dread of bedclothes, these lingering
doubts that we could never be who they say we are, our over-
sensitivity to the scent of leaves
burning by the roadside, all conspire to reveal the tale

our mother—if that's who she really is—
has carefully hidden from us: the truth replete, so we're told,
with contradictions. And the fact that we
have never caught her in one is the best sign of well-rehearsed

deception. Surely what we imagine
regularly and with such clarity cannot merely be
a product of the imagination.
This darkened street that comes before we sleep, the dull thud that sounds

so much like pulsations of the middle
ear, the cat-like moans of illicit desire must rise from somewhere
deep within us, the phantom limb of lives
cut short by horrors we are still unready to acknowledge.

Somewhere close a man is being beaten.
He speaks in a language we have never heard. Is he our father?
The night air insults us with its coldness.
Is it a trace of forced marches through trees shaped like bayonets?

Why could they (who?) not leave us alone?
Why must we cringe at the touch of parents? How could they show us
such marks of affection that we almost
can taste love flow like blood from the unopened wound of our mouth?

David Bergman

CAPTAIN FRED HANKEY OF THE GUARD, BIBLIOPHILE

That few had actually seen his library
        (and those who had were not
        disappointed) served but to increase
its fame within the small circle
                of like-minded bibliophiles.

A disciple of Sade, whose manuscripts
            he acquired when they
        made their way, not to the auction block—
that crude guillotine of commerce—
                but to the paneled rooms where deals

were cut with stiletto speed and precision;
            he sought only accounts
        of abduction and imprisonment,
masters dismembering their maids,
                slave girls lashed and fiercely buggered

whole harems slaughtered by their lusty viziers,
            the shrieks of pain and joy
        as women learned to their sad delight
the limits of their sumptuous bodies
                through the exercise of desires

not their own. He had made a study of it.
            His assiduity
        was legendary, but even such
prowess in collecting would not
                have brought the respect of colleagues

had not each volume been expertly bound
            (only he knew the shop),
        not in calf or Moroccan leather,
but in the priceless skins of girls
                preferable still alive when flayed.

When he and Sir Richard met, which was not
        infrequent, he renewed
    each time his request that Burton bring
him back from Africa some skins
            for which he'd pay quite dearly.

Whether the strips came from back or thigh appears
        not to have affected
    his estimation of their value;
each site would do as long as done
            while they were alive through its doing.

What he most desired was the luster of agony
        so he could imagine
    their cold sweat pouring from the spine:
with such bindings he had no need
            to open a volume to gain

the pleasures he was after, merely pulling
        one off the shelf ever
    so gently—and no one was gentler
than he (with his books)—just that tug
            was sometimes enough to produce

the electric shock that ran from his finger
        tips down into his groin
    before transfusing through his entire
body a sort of radiant
            glow: life's true bounty.

"Content!" he would joke over brandy with those
        connoisseurs he allowed
    to his preserve reached from behind glass
doors. "Content is for the vulgar;
            I judge a book by its cover."

Bill Berkson

EXTREME PATIENCE

Of those who, believing the world would end that
day, assembled on one member's front porch and sat,
waiting in the event that this should occur—it hasn't,
and at sunset they get back up and disperse to
separate houses until called when next to witness
such desirable oblivion.

SIGNS

A bird in a cage murders itself because it is not a metaphor—
& upon slaying itself it slaughters the cult of lamentation.

I eat it.

It is a broken tree. I am a furnace. My eyes are
saddles & I watch my neighbors set the woods on fire.

The dream in the dream:
charred bodies fall out of the sky
over Texas.

I have a clock made of paper.
It is always 10:10

My language does not have academic sanction
but is dragged down a dirt road by a pick-up truck
filled with high octane gasoline.

My wound is as thick as rope. My wound is a tear from left temple
& eye to groin to knee to right large toe.
It is a snake, an initiation.

The dream in the dream:
A river of toads & bone
saying the rain

(every dream is a kind of coffin, a mythological death as deep as
the dark. A place where we can only blink the world out in signs
—inventions doing unintended things before collapse.)

I am a muscled butterfly with an afro!
Why are there so many coyotes in my yard?
I touch the sky & all the birds disappear!
Why can't the barber cut my hair right?

I want to break the neck off the steeple
& crush the lice in the colonies & the colonial.

I'm so tired of Rome.
I'm so tired of the man on the oatmeal.
I'm so tired of the Uncle on the rice.

I'm sick of your sports.
Where the fuck are all the Indians?

I'm tired. I walked in the woods, trees tried to sell me stocks & bonds.
The water in the river was infected with noise & self-hatred.

My neighbors believe their children look like ice cream.
America is a boat carved in Braille.

Mishima once wrote about a man who beat a peacock to death because
it was beautiful—yeah, it was a short story.

I live in the country now & sometimes I want to beat nature
to death—but I can't.

In 1943 (what a year!) Artaud walked into a more humane mental
institution in Rodez—His worldly possessions consisted of the
following:

1 passport
1 paper knife
1 file

I need to lighten my load.

Dream in the dream:
My lover walking the length of a chopstick,
out from a bowl of noodles & soup,
small tart breasts the color of rosebuds,
calibrates my language & walks into my mouth
like candy. I must be careful with her tiny bones.

Now I am on her tongue, a foreign language.

Large airplane impossibly round circles the room.

A cannibal is edible. A cannibal is edible. A cannibal is a flower.
I refuse to be a gun & hide the television in the oven.

Corona is so far away. Avenue C & Flatbush are lonelier than any
                                                        mountain.
Sometimes I just miss the smell.

II.

Recipe for invention:

meat   meat   meat

The breath of the open road is littered with attack dogs & fences.
We are charged so much to help maintain its regression
into tyranny.

There is no underworld.
I will spend my time reinventing affection in the hot curves of my wife,
her warm exhale almost making sleep the perfect invitation.

I balance the dark & the light
temper the fuse in the Juggernaut

& reveal the true power of the poem
(that's right, poetry does nothing)
the inability to be used & the ability to endure any war—

III.

Chuang-Tzu 400 B.C.:

> *Do not be the possessor of fame. Do not be the storehouse of schemes. Do not take over the function of things. Do not be the master of knowledge. Personally realize the infinite to the highest degree and travel in the realm of which there is no sign. Exercise fully what you have received from Nature without any subjective viewpoint. In one word be absolutely vacuous.*
>
> *The mind of the perfect man is like a mirror. It does not lean forward or backward in its response to things. It responds to things but conceals nothing of its own. Therefore it is able to deal with things without injury to its reality.*

Nothing can conquer the world.
I refuse to be a gun.
Consciousness is insomnia.
I will not be defined.

GENETICALLY MODIFIED FOOD FOR THOUGHT
(Ode to Albert Flynn DeSilver)

No GOVERNMENT HEALTH WARNING in my grey field
with *de*fences all torn down; still, Albert Flynn
DeSilver wanders round, flicking like a switch
to automatic love-affair in the underground;
illuminating my darkest rooms.

How long has it been?

No warning;
No lonely tilting sigh of a sign, like a
scarecrow shot by loneliness; no dead dog's
shaggy carpet rolled out against the earth
one last time. No yellow-bricked road. No
loss: When I was a child, I was stared at
by a clown who wouldn't smile.

Mary Burger

THE SMARTEST MAN IN THE WORLD

The smartest man in the world isn't you.

The kindest man in the world isn't you.

There is a happy man, happy in his work, who makes many happy in the work he does, this is his work, he makes many happy, he is happy doing this.

There is a happy man. He is a little shaggy, loosely combed and trimmed. He is a little baggy, pants a little wide and sleeves too long. Sometimes he looks right at you and sometimes he looks around. He is happy in his work of making many others happy.

There are some men who are considered markers of how to be, this is so, though not every marker is a man.

It was hard, keeping quiet for so long. To watch this man who was happy. His happiness made others believe if they did what he did, they might be happy too. This is a folk tale. It tells a tale of people, it is a tale for people to tell. He was happy in the minor key and happy in the bright. His bright keys were for dancing and his dark keys were for holding still. Everyone, all the people, needed both. People needed dancing and they needed holding still.

It was hard, keeping quiet for so long. It was hard, knowing one was not the smartest man in the world, or a man at all. There were so many who would say they were. There were so many who would see each other die to say they were, men or the smartest men.

The smartest man is a shadow we emerge from. We are unspoiled by the absence of light, the momentary passing of something cold.

He is mournful, this happy man. He mourns the sorrow that he sees or that belongs to him. This man makes a space for mourning that is a small but complicated space.

IT'S SIMPLY A MATTER OF PHYSICS

Although I would like the attention of feminists, this is not primarily about feminism. I am not a feminist, although I know a few. I am not an "-ist" of any kind, just an individual with ideas I have learned or developed throughout my long life. I have read none of the books, but we can't avoid knowing about feminism.

It so happens that none of the women I know, including feminists, are aware of the basic energies that create and sustain all life. *That's* what interests me and I hope may you.

It's like this: The entire universe—as far as we three-dimensional, earth-bound creatures can know it—is constructed on the fusion of male and female energy—from the largest planet to the tiniest cell in our bodies—in every living thing. That is, life is possible from the combustion of positive (electric) and negative (magnetic) forces. (Of course, you understand that "negative" is here meant in the electricity connotation, that which isn't active but holds power.) It does not indicate "weakness"; it represents *reserve force*.

All of us have both of these polarities within us in varying degrees; some women have more Yang (masculine-electric), while some men have more Yin (feminine-magnetic). For instance, my daughter has more Yang and her husband more Yin. A salesman at the door selling cookware will aim for my daughter. She will point him to her husband, the chef. Someone selling fishing gear, on the other hand, will be directed to the wife. They are lucky to have found each other and have been married for thirty years. Think about it.

I don't know if all Suffragettes were endowed with more Yang, but they stirred up what they had to do the job that needed doing. Since then, women have asserted their Yang energy to affect some areas in our traditional male-oriented society that have resulted in better adjustments, such as equal pay for equal work, etc.

In non-tropical climates when winter comes, all of nature appears to die. Magnetic energy has replaced the electric almost entirely. Winter is thus considered the most spiritual season of the year, capped by the solstice. This is probably why the myths of the birth of Jesus placed that event here. (He had to be born on 21 March—the cusp of Pisces and Aries, the Alpha and Omega—never mind.)

Although in winter all energy in nature seems suspended, dormant, quiet, we all know such is not the case; the magnetic, feminine energy in the earth is building and nurturing new life with a tremendous force that explodes into glorious electric exhibitionistic male action in spring. (Aries is a fire sign.)

When the magnetic contacts the electric, it gives off this power; combustion occurs, a spark is lit, and force is generated into action. This process causes a planet to rotate, a car to move, a light bulb to glow, a plant to grow and a new animal or human to be conceived.

In our bodies the positive, electrical pole is represented by acids, the magnetic by alkalis. For action to take place, the right balance of these forces must be present to create little explosions of electrical life-force. (Some savants believe this is what "God" is.) The tiniest cell in our or any body is an electric battery in a state of combustion; our whole body is electrically polarized for action.

The acids are in the muscles, the alkali is in the blood *which holds and carries the power to these muscles.* Geddit? When we are alive and kicking, the two are in balance. At death the pole that separates them is withdrawn; the acid floods the alkali, and the whole mechanism becomes static. (The "male" acts.)

In Genesis, Adam symbolizes the positive, electric, intellectual left-brain attributes of Mankind. But he is not complete. He needs the balance of an emotional, feeling, imaginative artsy side, too. The King James translation is that he took a rib and produced Eve. I prefer the translation that says he took a "place near his heart". Actually, what he did was "project" the thought of her into materiality, something we all did in former times and which some Yogis claim to do today. So now the electric and the magnetic are joined. And—think about it—isn't it always our emotions that get us into trouble? Poor Eve; she made every woman from then on the guilty party. Of course, as always, in the end it comes down to sex—the serpent, the apple—well, that's another story.

I just wish more women understood that the feminine, the Yin, is a far more powerful force than the Yang, but you have to be subtle and clever to use it properly to your advantage without destroying the power of Yang to act, which is essential to you, too. Today, many women want to reverse these roles; they want to be the active, aggressive force and obtain recognition for themselves as women empowered the same as men. That hints a teeny bit of ego—"Look at me—I'm a woman, and anything he can do I can do better."

So many women in the past have become famous for what they achieved as women, although it may have taken longer. The Brontë sisters accepted the situation, played the game, and in the end are celebrated as women authors. The two "Georges" went further and wore masculine clothing, but as time went on, all women who are celebrated today found a way to get what they deserved without bashing men. Men do have their uses and equal rights, too. Sex clinicians record a huge rise in impotence since the rise of feminism. Some men are confused as to just what their role is and seek to preserve some self-respect and approval with other men. I think this is so sad—there aren't enough men to go around as it is. Have a heart, ladies!

I personally eat up chivalry with a big spoon! Of course, I'm strong enough to open a car door and pull out my own chair. (My brother: "Whatsa matter? You got a broken arm?") But I always felt men were doing those little niceties as a sign of *respect* for me as a *woman*—a creature who not only took care of some of his needs and inspired him, and one who could build a new human being in her tummy. (I read some place the male sperm is imperfect; the female egg perfect. True?) I celebrate men's positive, active pole, and I sure miss a handyman around the house—even though I'm a pretty good carpenter and have a mountain of tools. Still, I have to trap a passing plumber to change a light bulb in the ceiling.

Another example: In astrology, Venus, the "evaluator" looks around at things, makes up her mind and then sends Mars out to kill it or love it. Think of a rocket. There sits the familiar form on its pad, inert. Inside is this motionless liquid, perfectly calm and quiet. Get that to touch him, and that rocket roars off into the wide blue yonder. Otherwise useless without that quiet magnetism.

As said, we all have both polarities within us, and both should be expressed in a balanced, appropriate way. The old saw that "behind every successful man is a woman" is no bad thing. Does it really matter if we forget the name of Abraham Lincoln's wife? We know he had that magnetic force with him, and HE is her reward—and the world's. That's why marriage was invented to have one of each force.

"Successful" women are not eliminated, unless it's self-glory they're after. (I'll bet there's a man lurking around somewhere—acting.) The essential power in women, then, is YIN. Without that Yin, men would be helpless. Give 'em a break, gals! (And curb that Yang when you want to seduce him—use your Yin, instead, and magnetize.)

Women are to BE—Men are to DO

Let's hear from Fran Landesman, that brilliant poet and lyricist. (She said I could.)

> I quite like men
> They're rather sweet.
> I like to give them things to eat.
> When they're not being
> Perfect swine
> They're nice with candlelight and wine.
>
> They have nice hands
> And charming necks
> And some of them are good at sex.
> My sympathies are feminist
> But I am glad that men exist.
>
> They warm me up
> When I am cold
> And one or two have hearts of gold
> They irritate me now and then
> But on the whole
> I quite like men.

FIN

A drawing I did of Jack from life — A copy.

Jack Kerouac. Drawing by Carolyn Cassady
Ink on Paper, San José, California 1956

"As to the drawing," says Carolyn Cassady, "I don't remember exactly the date. Probably when he was living with us in San José and working on the railroad. That would be 1956. Only times we had to sit around together for any length of time."

Courtesy Carolyn Cassady Collection

Original manuscript image of Neal Cassady's August 10, 1948 letter to Bill Tomson.

Courtesy of Carolyn Cassady

August 10, 1948

Dear Willy Boy;
      Here, my sweet, at long last, is my much-late latest lyric to my
fabulous younger-blood-brother. I do feel most contrite that having
been preoccupied with great, growling, purple-pasted, sombre life of
late, I had no time for you. Instead, like you I'm sure, I've been
growing into wisdom. Now, I'm wise; let me speak, once again, to you,
my dear Bill. I do fear the natural course of things have had a tend-
ency to deviate us from the mutual direction we once shared. Conver-
sly, however, this sense of loss is good in that I think about, and
feel toward, you with much more gleeful fondness; with a glowing
awareness of your touch—I say simply; Brother Bill.
      Now, listen here, you mustn't start the same foolishness most of
the Denver all-bright lads do. Let's have no watered-down "second-
youth" spent in wasted effort txxxixx traveling-big, living-big,
acting-big. What I'm saying is; your youthful pure emotion is passed,
life tastes jaded, your reactions are sterile, your big-souled desires
and big-headed opinions refuse to fuse into reality. You blame all
else but yourself; mother, (other stupid peoples) Denver, (other stupid
places--that aren't big) women, (no mind; stupid, no soul; more stupid)
everything becomes stupid--but, you. The one phase of understanding
you know does not constitute all understanding,i.e.-use insight to be-
come, not wallow in prideful insight and just be. You must come to
see you are nothing, then, grow into something. Ahem, Ahem, for a
good example, follow your big brother Neal L. into hell--I used wo-
men, tea and psychology--what'll you use?
      All kiding aside Bill, I'm leading a great, perfectly pearly life.
How are you coming along? Are you sure of your new gal? Do you have
the glee and joy of a rock of Gibralter in your intelgent guts?
(Don't let the huge foolish triteness everywhere about you come to be
a cause of frustration and drag to you; sleep with Dante, feel with
Shakespeare, work with Eliot and Auden, play with Goethe and Proust,
sin with Dostoievsky and Kaufka, suffer with Baudelaire and Rimbaud.
Do the same with Art; study and see all Paris 50 years ago, Van Gogh,
Cezanne, Gauguin, L-Autrec, Matisse, Picasso, etc) Do the same with
music; with your knowledge of Western music,(not hillbilly, of course,
but, western swing--big bands, semi-commercial players from James to
Ziggy Elman, Benny Carter to Johnny Hodges, J. Teagarden to Kai Wind-
ing, Gene Krupa to Shelly Mane, Fats Waller to Errol Garner, Woody
Herman to Benny Goodman etc.) your have a natural tendency to dig
the half-beat, or, off-beat, (witness cf old harmonizing on two O'clock
Jump) now, forget this western stuff and convert your rhythm to an
intellectual feeling for Eastern Jazz; personified by, Dizzy, Howard
MaGee, Buck Clayton, Chico Alvarez, Earl Payton, etc. on the trumpets;
Lester Young, Coleman Hawkins, Dexter Gorden, Illinois Jacquet, Vido
Musso, Wardell Grey, on the tenor Saxophones; Charlie Parker, Willie
Smith, King Perry, Boots Mussilli, etc, on the Alto Saxs; Bill Harris,
(this Harris is the only good Bop trombone player, so, after him the
rest of the slush pipes could be played be half a dozen men) is the
lead trombone; The Clarinet section is difficult also because all
the good men are deserting this instrument for the better sounding
and more vibrant instrument--the sax, however, a kid named Matlock
is bopin' good clarinet still; The drums are still being dominated
by the great Shelly Mane, although he's modified his style and left
Stan Kenton, there is noone on the horizon to beat him, unless we
could dig up some of the wild, mad Calypso tea-head drummers; Guitar
leader is Barney Kessel, next comes Al Harris or even Dave Barbour;
Lionel Hampton on the Vibes; Eddie Stravinski on the Bass; Stan
Wrightsman on the piano(he's a greatly underated French player, who
went there a few years ago because nothing good was being done in
America) and for xxxxxx arranger; Cameron. This quick, brief re-
sumé of players has left out accidentally such talented men as:
Charlie Shavers on trumpet, Harry Carney on Sax, Irvin Verret on
trombone, Pee Wee Russel on Clarinet, Catlett, T.Otis, Nick Fatool etc,
on drums. (over)

"This is a letter Neal wrote to Bill Tomson—the guy who introduced me to Neal in Denver. Bill's daughter allows me to publish it. She provided it."

—Carolyn Cassady, 28 June 2004

Editor's Note: The [*sic*]s have been omitted in order to preserve the experience of Neal Cassady writing in his rush.

August 10, 1948

Dear Willy Boy:

Here, my sweet, at long last, is my much-late latest lyric to my fabulous younger-blood-brother. I do feel most contrite that having been preoccupied with great, growling, purple-pasted, sombre life of late, I had no time for you. Instead, like you I'm sure, I've been growing into wisdom. Now, I'm wise; let me speak, once again, to you, my dear Bill. I do fear the natural course of things have had a tendency to deviate us from the mutual direction we once shared. Conversly, however, this sense of loss is good in that I think about, and feel toward, you with much more gleeful fondness; with a glowing awareness of your touch--I say simply: Brother Bill.

Now, listen here, you mustn't start the same foolishness most of the Denver all-bright lads do. Let's have no watered-down "second-youth" spent in wasted effort traveling-big, living-big, acting-big. What I'm saying is; your youthful pure emotion is passed, life tastes jaded, your reactions are sterile, your big-souled desires and big-headed opinions refuse to fuse into reality. You blame all else but yourself: mother, (other stupid peoples) Denver, (other stupid places--that aren't big) women, (no mind; stupid, no soul; more stupid) everything becomes stupid--but, you. The one phase of understanding you know does not constitute all understanding, i.e.-use insight to become, not wallow in prideful insight and just be. You must come to see you are nothing, then, grow into something. Ahem, Ahem, for a good example, follow your big brother Neal L. into hell--I used women, tea and psychology--what'll you use?

All kiding aside Bill, I'm leading a great, perfectly pearly life. How are you coming along? Are you sure of your new gal? Do you have the glee and joy of a rock of Gibralter in your intelligent guts? (Don't let the huge foolish triteness everywhere about you come to be a cause of frustration and drag to you; sleep with Dante, feel with Shakespeare, work with Eliot and Auden, play with Goethe and Proust, sin with Dostoievsky and Kaufka, suffer with Baudelaire and Rimbaud. Do the same with Art; study and see all Paris 50 years ago, Van Gogh, Cezanne, Gauguin, L-Autrec, Matisse, Picasso, etc.) Do the same with music; with your knowledge of Western music, (not hillbilly, of course, but, western swing--big bands, semi-commercial players from James to Ziggy Elman, Benny Carter to Johnny Hodges, J. Teagarden to Kai Winding, Gene Krupa to Shelly Mane, Fats Waller to Errol Garner, Woody Herman to Benny Goodman etc.) your have a natural tendency to dig the half-beat, or, off-beat, (witness of old harmonizing on two O'clock Jump) now, <u>forget</u> this western stuff and convert your rhythm to an intellectual feeling for Eastern Jazz; personified by, Dizzy, Howard MaGee, Buck Clayton, Chico Alvarez, Earl Payton, etc. on the trumpets; Lester Young, Coleman Hawkins, Dexter Gordon, Illinois Jacquet, Vido Musso, Wardell Grey, on the tenor Saxophones; Charlie Parker, Willie Smith, King Perry, Boots Mussilli, etc, on the Alto Saxs; Bill Harris, (this Harris is the only good Bop trombone player, so, after him the rest of the slush pipes could be played be half a dozen men) is the lead trombone; The Clarinet section is difficult also because all the good men are deserting this instrument for the better sounding and more vibrant instrument--the sax, however, a kid named Matlock is bopin' good clarinet still; The drums are still being dominated by the great Shelly Mane, although he's modified his style and left Stan Kenton, there is noone on the horizon to beat him, unless we could dig up some of the wild, mad Calypso tea-head drummers; Guitar leader is Barney Kessal, next comes Al Harris or even Dave Barbour; Lionel Hampton on the Vibes; Eddie Stravinski on the Bass; Stan Wrightsman on the piano (he's a greatly underated French player, who went there a few years ago because nothing good was being done in America) and for arranger: Cameron. This quick, brief resumé of players has left out accidentally such talented men as: Charlie Shavers on trumpet, Harry

Carney on Sax, Irvin Verret on trombone, Pee Wee Russel on Clarinet, Catlett, T.Otis, Nick Fatool etc. on drums. Once you are in touch and familiar with modern music and its place, its problems, its potentialities etc. you must then dig the classics; Mozart, Beethoven, first; Stravinsky, Mahluer, second; then, flit about from one to another; one composer to another, one century to another, past masters to present masters (like Ellington, Kenton, Gillespie) etc. By that time you'll have evolved your own real tastes and desires, and perhaps, do something yourself in furthering todays music.

Just as you are being advised to really dig Literature, Art, Music by me, so too, you must delve into theatre just as fully. The art of drama, dear Bill, is our mutual love, with, perhaps, literature a close second. Of late I find theatre, more and more, looming up as a practical medium for me to work with. Of course, we differ in that you think in terms of acting and picturing acting motifs; you fantasize yourself as a Barrymorian character with overtones of Falstaffian and Don Juanian caracteristics: whereas I think more in terms of the play and directing motifs; I fantasize myself into Shakespearian struggles with plot, Andersonian concern with scenes, Hitchcockian methods of capturing Wellesian moments. Joyce-like dialouge. etc. I have envisioned a Maughm-like third act for a great play we could stage in my kitchen; with Carolyn handling the costumes and scenery etc. me directing and producing and casting and writing the play, you would be the lead and portray a faustian soul lost in the clutches of a negro whore. It's a beautiful thing with everything in it, Faust-like enigma, Human Bondage-like suffering, Wolfe-like scenes of rich social people, Richard Wright-like (with porgy and bess overtones) into the negro soul, Martha Graham-like symbolized dance routines. etc. etc.

Please, now Bill, no accusations of verbosity from you, I've just been rattling away in a tone of careless gleeful abstractions to let you know I feel close enough to you, once again, to be allowed to use mixed metaphors, vague foolishness etc. in my excess fondness and drunken (I'm not) goodfellowship toward you. You warm the cockles of my heart, indeed you do.

More practical now; first, there are no apt's in Frisco at present, at least, noneunder 70 a month. At best there are some fairly good light housekeeping rooms for 10-15 dollars a week. Of course, as winter approches things will ease off a bit and a nice apt. for about 50 a month could, with worthy effort, be found. However, the problem of a place to live is secondary and always managed somehow. So, let's consider the prime problem; work. All jobs out here are union, with many of them having training periods without pay (Standard oil, for instance). The grim fact is that even dishwashing is controlled and has no openings. In fact, Frisco has the strange paradox of needing no working men, but rather, all openings here are not based on necessary things like industry, commerce etc., instead, jobs are produced by luxury or superfluous needs---salesmen! book, magazines, lingerie, gadgets, brushes, insurance (low-class), drug etc. Also there are openings for white-collar jobs, banks, offices, department stores IF you have had experience enough to qualify. Thinking now of you as an individual, there are no book stores, no truck driving, no parking lot;-- actually, Bill, as I sit here trying to enumerate your skills and job qualifications, I can think of none. Do you realize how little you have worked, and how much this town bases you on references, previous jobs etc.?

(the typewriter just broke) Oh, I need no reminding of your willingness to try — to be quite honest — I truly believe you need to come out here & do your absolute best toward making your own way. I mean making your own way on all levels — work, play, sex, creative outlet, &, in general, making yourself indispensible to as many people & places as is in your power. This means not gadding about in all the hip places, with all the hep people. Rather, I ask you to

(Page 3)

"*I suspect the missing page would have been Neal's current adventures, which are covered in the new book of his letters due out in August from Penguin.*"

—Carolyn Cassady, 28 June 2004

Original manuscript image of Neal Cassady's August 10, 1948 letter (second page).

Courtesy of Carolyn Cassady

Once you are in touch and familiar with modern music and its place,
its problems, its potentialities etc. you must then dig the classics;
Mozart, Beethoven, first; Stravinsky, Mahluer, second; then, flit about
from one to another; one composer to another, one century to another,
past masters to present masters (like Ellington, Kenton, Gillespie)
etc. By that time you'll have evolved your own real tastes and desires,
and perhaps, do something yourself in futhering todays music.

Just as you are being advised to really dig Literature, Art, Music
by me, so too, you must delve into theatre just as fully. The art of
drama, dear Bill, is our mutual love, with, perhaps, literature a close
second. Of late I find theatre,more and more,looming up,as a practical
medium for me to work with. Of course, we differ in that you think
in terms of acting and picturing acting motifs; you fantasize your-
self as a Barrymorian character with overtones of Falstaffian and
Don Juanian caracteristics: whereas I think more in terms of the play
and directing motifs; I fantasize myself into Shakespearian struggles
with plot, Andersonian concern with scenes, Hitchcockian methods of
capturing Wellesian moments, Joyce-like dialouge, etc. I have envis-
ioned a Maughm-like third act for a great play we could stage in my
kitchen; with Carolyn handling the costumes and scenery etc. me dir-
ecting and producing and casting and writing the play, you would be
the lead and protray a faustian soul lost in the clutches of a negro
whore. It's a beautiful thing with everything in it, Faust-like
enigma, Human Bondage-like suffering, Wolfe-like scenes of rich social
people, Richard Wright-like (with porgy and bess overtones) into the
negro soul, Martha Graham-like symbolized dance routines. etc. etc.

Please, now Bill, no accusations of verbosity from you, I've
just been rattling away in a tone of careless gleeful abstractions
to let you know I feel close enough to you,once again,to be allowed
to use mixed metaphores, vague foolishness etc. in my excess fondness
and drunken (I'm not) goodfellowship toward you. You warm the cockles
of my heart, indeed you do.

More practical now; first, there are no apt's in Frisco at pre-
sent, at least, noneunder 70 a month. At best there are some fairly
good light housekeeping rooms for 10-15 dollars a week. Of course,
as winter approches things will ease off a bit and a nice apt. for
about 50 a month could,with worthy effort, be found. However, the
problem of a place to live is secondary and always managed somehow.
So, lets consider the prime problem; work. All jobs out here are
union, with many of them having training periods without pay (Standard
oil, for instance). The grim fact is that even dishwashing is
controlled and has no openings. In fact, Frisco has the strange
paradox of needing no working men, but rather, all openings here
are not based on necessary things like industry, commerce etc.,
instead, jobs are produced by luxury or superfluous needs---salesmen!
book, magazines, lingerie, gadgets, brushes, insurance (low-class),
drug etc. Also there are openings for white-collar jobs, banks,
offices, department stores IF you have had experience enough to
qualify. Thinking now of you as an individual, there are no
book stores, no truck driving, no parking lot;-- actually, Bill,
as I sit here trying to enumerate your skills and job qualifications,
I can think of none. Do you realize how little you have worked,
and how much this town bases you on references, previous jobs etc.?
(the typewriter just broke) But, I need no reminding of your willingness
to try — to be quite honest — I truly believe You need to come out here
+ do your absolute best toward making your own way. I mean making
your own way on all levels — work, play, sex, creative outlet,
+, in general, making yourself indispensible to as many people +
places as is in your power. This means not gadding about
in all the hip places, with all the hip people. Rather, I ask you to
(Page 3)

Andrei Codrescu

E.U., OR THE POETRY OF MENUS
For Mark Steinberg

and in Champaign-Urbana
at Bacaro
with Bulgarian historian, Hungarian sociologist,
midwestern ethno-musicologist,
host Slavicist
and Korean minder
(I go nowhere without them)
I am introduced to a wholly new
part of the cow: "hanger steak"
hitherto unknown but tenderer
the native menu poet claims than filet mignon
better than the boar also on the menu
shot in Texas by George W.
and garnished with blue red and white
tendrils or mushrooms!
I lost you at the tendrils, poet.
The Slavicist: me, by the mushrooms.
The poetry of menus grows more complex
and its performers are the envy of the world
and when the cow's newly discovered
"hanger steak" (somewhere between
shoulder and flank, how it slipped by
all these years I can't imagine) arrives
it is small and compact and firm on its
bed of dime-sized burned potato chips
it is tender awright but not *more* tender
than filet mignon or boar or anything
tenderized by pounding and marinating
& I ask the Bulgarian historian

How are our socialist pigs different
from all other pigs? Why, they have more parts,
she says, and they surrender them more willingly.
Bingo. And the European Union wants
Romanian pigs sedated, a culturally
and gastronomically unwise move
in a country where the taste of terror
is worth the whole price of admission
and the poetry of menus still an oral form

Leonard Cohen

THE DRUNKARD BECOMES GENDER-FREE

This morning I woke up again
I thank my Lord for that
The world is such a pigpen
That I have to wear a hat

I love the Lord I praise the Lord
I do the Lord forgive
I hope I won't be sorry
For allowing Him to live

I know you like to get me drunk
And laugh at what I say
I'm very happy that you do
I'm lonely every day

I'm angry at the angel
Who pinched me on the thigh
And made me fall in love
With every woman passing by

I know they are your sisters
And your daughters and your wives
But even tho' they live at home
They all lead double lives

It's fun to run to heaven
When you're off the beaten track
But G-d is such a monkey
When you've got Him on your back

G-d is such a monkey
And He's such a woman too
SHe's such a place of nothing
SHe's such a face of you

May SHe crash into your temple
And look out thru' your eyes
And make you fall in love
With everybody you despise

Billy Collins

HEIGHT

From the roof of a very tall building,
the people on the street
are said to take on the appearance of ants,

but I have been up here so long,
gazing down over the concrete lip,
that the ants below have begun to resemble people.

Look at that one lingering
near a breadcrumb on the curb,
the one who reminds me of my brother-in-law.

And the lovely young ant
in the light summer dress
with the smooth, ovoid face,

the one heading up the lamp post—
does she not look like my favorite cousin
with her glad eyes and her pulled back hair?

Surely, an ant with the face
of my mother and another with the posture
of my father are soon to go staggering by.

And there you are,
the one I think of most often,
carrying some small thing in your beautiful pincers.

hungry.

so here's the story. we were in au bon pain. there we were, the three of us, sitting at a table. her. me. the muffin. me, the muffin, and her. the muffin. she stared at the muffin. i stared at her. the muffin stared at the ceiling. the ceiling stared at the muffin. i stared at her. she stared at the muffin. we couldn't take it anymore. she broke the muffin in half. now there were two muffins. she stared at the muffins. the muffins stared at the ceiling. the ceiling stared at the muffins. i stared at her. smaller, i said. make them smaller. three muffins. four muffins. five muffins. six muffins. she stared at the muffins. the muffins stared at the ceiling. the ceiling stared at the muffins. i stared at her. smaller, she said. smaller. seven muffins, eight muffins, nine muffins, ten muffins. muffins and muffins and muffins. twenty muffins, thirty muffins, forty muffins. smaller, she said. smaller. fifty muffins, sixty muffins, seventy muffins. the crumbs scattered all over the table. eighty muffins, ninety muffins, one hundred muffins. smaller, she said. smaller. smaller. smaller. muffins. muffins. muffins. i stared at her. she stared at the muffins. there were hundreds of crumbs. the crumbs stared at the ceiling. the ceiling stared at the crumbs. the lady with the umbrella stared at us. the man in the window stared at the crumbs. the crumbs stared at the ceiling. the ceiling stared at the crumbs. she stared at the muffins. i stared at her. eat, i said. too many, she said. the crumbs stared at the ceiling. the ceiling stared at the crumbs. she stared at the muffins. i stared at her. the waitress asked her if she would like another muffin. muffins, she said, muffins. crumbs, i said, they are crumbs. no, she said, they are muffins. the crumbs stared at the ceiling. the ceiling stared at the crumbs. she stared at the muffins. i stared at her.

Holly Crawford

ONE RED UMBRELLA

A society, as it becomes less and less able,
in the course of its development,
to justify its particular forms,
important issues are left untouched.

A political kidnapper had me in front of an AK-47
and very much wanted to pull the trigger.
Did you ever think of the zillions of leaves
that come into our view in the fall?
Every fall, every year?

TWO TRICYCLES

I went to the opera for a nickel.
While I was there, over two hundred people,
mostly civilians, were killed.

How strange that this could happen to a chronically healthy child.
We'd thought most diseases had been covered by shots or outgrown.

Narrowing and raising to the expression of an absolute
in which all relatives and contradictions would be either resolved
or beside the point. We must not be deceived
by superficial phenomena.

Victor Hernández Cruz

SYLVIA REXACH 1

Along with what you respire from the air
Is a voice with her words,
salty and right out of the sea.
The horizon what the whole eye
can eat,
Clouds which we confuse with mountains,
distance buildings Santurce, Rio Piedras
antennas upon everything her songs
are pouring like rich tamarindo.
The entire oval of the island imbibes,
the coquettish flames
The florid arboreal gives birth to
so much possibility of encounter,
insisting like the waves of the sea.
The sand we lay upon is sound,
something so soil
so purple
so moisture.
Mountains suffer their separation
in the panorama of sex,
Roble trees shine as if in orgasm,
the roots of the plants receive the
seeds of other planets
And they occasion to grow with us,
listen to the vegetation that travels
with the guitar,
A call and response to the hurt,
gold tooth gypsy's drink café
at la Bobonera.
A chorus repeats the humidity
two spoons of sugar pour into
the black liquid of night
dance with the saucers
bitter occupation.

Sea shells feel the lyrical pain,
the woman composing a butterfly
She wrote on gardenia petals
with the sharp pencil of her soul.
Oblivion returns to the memory
Through those journeys where
the captain of the boat sailed,
a ship lost in blue desire.
Her metaphors of liquid
tongue upon the flesh,
the bolero is in Jupiter,
From the bay of San Juan
we see its sixteen moons
Full.
We are the text of lament
she inquired so much of,
the wound opened and luminous.

From an open window
a woman sits
She is made of jasmine and salt,
A flower of fire instinct of the birds,
she jots down words which
have eyes
They stare back up at who
writes them into melody.
Her hands are rosy
spilling a lilac ink,
Clouds of tenderness
outside the window,
It rains one more time
upon our memories.

Study of a Suffering Man. Painting by Colin Askey (www.colinaskey.com)
Oil on Canvas, Paris, France 2002

Courtesy Colin Askey Collection

AN OLD MAN SEES A YOUNG BOY
(*MUTANT CANNIBALS HOME TO ROOST*)

Every village green like Times Square
each fourteen cleancut choirboy becomes
a potential assassin—a slow afternoon
walk to grocery store mainlines adrenaline.

Neighbourhood Watch almost too scared to
watch anymore but still voyeurs cable tv
beyond tightly closed curtain sanctuaries;
vigilantes tracked by sociopathic toddlers.

Pre-emptive strike where Herod left off
—psychic bullrushes torched forever—
in the words of the immortal Hesterhouse
"Do it to them before they do it to you".

Schools out and armies of muggers
arsonists vandals glue-brained smack-
crazed monsters simultaneously hit mean city
streets grim town squares raw rural retreats.

Lowlife playgrounds host plagues
of self-destruct nihilistic energy
kickstart kids child crazies teenytot
toughs young yobs playschool psychos.

Schools holding operations open slammers
or universities of pre-pubic crime crammers.
Public show a baby hoodlum or throw
away its already menacing infant key.

Swift had a plan W. C. Fields an insight
into each issue of our unsafe sex
that grows away and slowly backtracks
raging to haunt stalk and devour us.

Tony Curtis

A FLEMISH LANDSCAPE

This mid-March snow
surprised the low lands
with its soft shroud
thrown over dark green and bare trees.

The unseasonable deaths
of birds and insects.

Pelted by snow
the ditched backseat of a car
is draped with icy ermine,
where a buttery girl
and her hunter
could be enthroned.

A clutter of crows
lifts from the copse
into the blank canvas.

MEDICINE FUCK DREAM

Children suing their parents had just come in vogue.
If I didn't conform
I'd never get laid.

A busted femur got me a trip to Bo Phut.
And, an ounce of alarming semen.

One *New Yorker* article suggested I stay put.
A breathy airplane no place
for someone in my condition.

Microscopic voices fawned over me.
Providing a base of loyalty
from which grotesque fireflies scammed cartons of brie.

They said the fever lasted
six point eight miles
along an icy beach front
from which I alone stared.

I made paths through, thru snow
with teaspoons and cigarette filters.
Wound my way back to Indianapolis and television.

Andrew Darlington

GURU OF THE NORTHERN LINE
(LONDON: THE POST-IRAQ SETTLEMENT)

phantom cop
with a real sub-machinegun
watches me slouch by as
spy-cameras switch and focus,
three suits tap lap-top encrypts
through Starbucks glass at me

tracking suspect poems
in my head, thermal-imaging
for unwise sympathies,
subversive syllables spooling
from my pockets,
incendiary thoughts
leaking in DNA-streams
of breath

as Cromwell watches pennants
across Westminster shadow
'the only good war is no war
the only bad peace is no peace'

but hey, Oliver,
if al-Qaeda don't get me
the state will . . .

     *   *   *

black mass throbbing square
in motion, if not in Movement,
ancient imperial streets still vibrant
with warm meat of new life,
paved with pizza-
pack, fast-food wrap

and a guru on the Northern Line
stands his turn in sandals and saffron
queuing in line for nirvana . . .

James Dean. Sketch by John Gilmore (www.johngilmore.com)
Oil on Canvas, East Hollywood, California 1955

"Jimmy visited my mother twice and read some of his poetry to her," says John Gilmore.
"My mother's apartment was west of L.A.'s Silverlake area, now called East Hollywood.
She'd been an actress in the 1930's. Jimmy once posed on a stool there while I sketched
him, supposedly reciting Alan Seeger's "I Have a Rendezvous with Death". His idea. This
was around Easter, 1955. When I had the skull sketched, the one he had the rendezvous
with, he said, "Make it laughing—'cause it's a joke.""

Courtesy Jonathan Gilmore Collection

Original manuscript image of James Dean's "Ode to a Tijuana Toilet" (May, 1955).

Courtesy of John Gilmore

ODE TO A TIJUANA TOILET*

(OR THE FAMOUS FUCK YOU
PROSAIC PRINCIPLE.)

Portrait of Jim & naked ass
in the mirror (from backstage
it is said: IT IS "MORBID!"
Is it MORIBUND it is asked,
Oh Great Crusty bowel of no end
SHOWING HIS BALLS TO THE WORLD
Is it Sebastian
yanking arrows out of his butt
Or the brave matador's shadow
the last moment in the mirror
IS IT THE FATHER $1/_2$
who cries it is the "MORBID SON"
THE ANSWER ARRIVES:
Fuck dad, dear dad, fuck you.
The lonely man who can't
get out
from the back of the mirror
Great puppet of the Other
O breathing life
to the dead on the sand
Dried sea weed that speaks
singing Italian Songs
On Patchen Place
to the caged girl
The body in a tin can
empty of the soul
The crow is crowing
and two becomes one

THE END

The pen is set aside,
the moving finger wrote
and now he takes a shit.

*James Dean's poem, "Ode to a Tijuana Toilet", composed in May, 1955, during the filming of *Rebel without a Cause*, erupted from a long estrangement from his father that began even before Dean's mother's untimely death. His father, Winton Dean, "Shipped me out," Dean would later tell me, "on the same train with my mother's body. She was being in a coffin and I was walking around but it was like I'd died, too, and was made into some asshole zombie."

Dean believed his father refused to see that his son had become a success ("Hey! I'm a *movie* star! Doesn't that mean *any*thing to you?"), or that Dean was someone important, someone to be reckoned with.

The "fuck you father" theme surfaced as well in Dean's most important film, *East of Eden* (the rejection by the father of the son—even the son's failure to bribe his father's love), and from his work in *Rebel Without a Cause* dealing with a father's failure to communicate with his son.

A drawing on a napkin (Googie's during the "nightwatch" era and long since lost), of a sombrero-wearing matador with over-sized balls, riding a motorcycle and holding a fuck-you finger aloft, accompanied this poem. "Patchen Place" [*sic*] refers to the House of Detention for Women on New York's Sixth Avenue and Greenwich Avenue. Woozy from too many beers in San Remo Café, Dean once danced on a street corner and sang, "O Solo Mio" to a young woman behind a barred window, almost getting himself thrown in the clinker. This poem of anger and rebellion pits Dean as a kind of Tijuana-style Garcia Lorca in the bullring of fame, an isolated warrior at odds with authority.

One of three poems typed width-wise on a yellow second sheet, the "Ode to a Tijuana Toilet" was given to me by Dean in Googie's, the other two poems passed to another friend, Jack Simmons, with Dean's comment that the "Ode" poem was "weighted" because it "carries a bigger turd . . . "

Riding motorcycles at three in the morning and winding up in Googie's —the so-called "nightwatch" era—was a short-lived period during the making of *Rebel Without a Cause*. Dean would often quote stanzas from Alan Seeger's poem, "I Have a Rendezvous with Death." Eartha Kitt, myself, Jack Simmons, occasionally Vampira of Ed Wood, Jr., fame, and a couple others on the sidelines of a "pecking order" associated with James Dean.

2005 marks the fiftieth anniversary of James Dean's death, and the fiftieth year since this poem was composed by Dean on an old Royal typewriter in Jack Simmons' apartment off Sunset Boulevard.

Simmons told Dean, "I'll get these poems published," but hoarded them in a manila envelope upon which Dean had written in pencil, "The classics to be revisited soon by James Dean". Four months later Dean was dead, at age twenty-four. All but "Ode to a Tijuana Toilet" has been lost.

John Gilmore
Hollywood, CA
Sep. 24, 2004

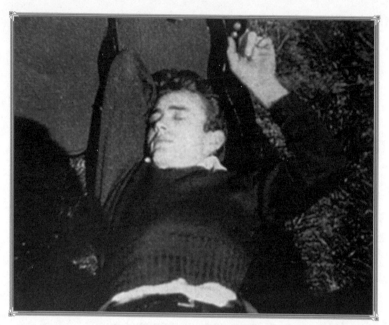

James Dean, New York City, 1953. Photo by John Gilmore. "This snapshot of Dean was in early Fall, 1953," says Gilmore, "in Manhattan's Central Park on a Sunday morning. He said, 'My church is the monkey house' in the park's zoo."

Photo courtesy Jonathan Gilmore Collection

John Gilmore, New York City, 1953. Photo by James Dean. "Dean's photo of me was taken with a Rollei," says Gilmore, "We'd just bopped off the subway where he'd been snapping pictures of people and crummy walls. This was on the stoop of a vacated building on Sixth Avenue (long-since Avenue of the Americas)."

Photo courtesy Jonathan Gilmore Collection

Albert Flynn DeSilver

THE STUNTED CONE

After Frédéric Louis Sauser

My head is conical
My pen,
My poems, all
conical
586 open letters of the hackneyed alphabet
each character a window-eye   crawl through

The drawl of car alarms
Church bells in North Beach
Muffled & gagged by motorcycle pipes
Flipping up Columbus's trash-bled asphalt
Hundreds of chrome suns swatting eyes blind
on the boulevards

Look at Luigi take swipes at the sky with his squeegee,
His smeared palette of windy gray
Goes drip in the street

All is antennae in the streets
Sprouting out of head, hair, and ear
Mouths shouting at themselves like
Bull-horns on hormones
Plucking skinny signals from knotted air

The clicking of heels are wood-
Peckers drilling for coins in the aluminum
Street lamps. The galloping of horses
Down Market Street—Its the Wells Fargo
Wagon Train. Money

Has been trampled under foot
Has been bought up and out of itself.
It used to be you burned a hole in your pocket,
Now both your thighs are in flames
Your bare hands hold holes

You must wear your gray latex
To handle the green fog

And still in Golden Gate Park
Great golden Dahlias blaze
Right through our great golden sadness
Thousands of square feet of Kentucky
Blue Grass is beholden to your chronic pain

The haggard bells of old trolleys
Still ping down on Powell.

Stop now! Let the breeze
pour through the tip
of your funneled geometry.

Peter James drew

JOHN WIENERS *MEMORIES OF YOU*

he happily paid for his poetry with
his health and heart

view the red sea
first from the right then
left,   can he see it as his death

         – his stop-n-shop notebook
               no elastic   /   elastic
                  plastic buttercup green

his   blue
shoes are   socks with
dirty   yellow faded
             lines

in his stop-n-shop notebook
his last poems at Orono
another envelope
when we shared a joint
it was so cold last night
when he died

          held in the hands of dreamers; the holds
                     are heavy
           …
           through clouds
           …
      drifting in the canals of heaven
           …
      burnt with memory of love
           …
      I want to swim in his rain
           …
     he throws his eyes into mine

FLUIDS ADMIN.

venal echo, two workers
slow to jump off surfaces, Atkins lo-carb
part one, digital hairspray cosseting
cocked shape of seltzer breeze
the other one is frightening us, maybe asks
do you believe in the enemy?
because,
a few of us would have raised our hands
repeat it, when the poor come to the door it is
Christ who comes,
breeze blows an ant into my room
lands like lint, crawl on my sheets, lose track of him
I used to pick my scabs as a child because
I thought they were bugs stuck to my skin

memorize buy by date, freeze by date, sit there date,
watch t.v. on a date, stock stir fry, the head hits the steering wheel,
horn sounds,
cut away to the next scene,
movie star lights in the bathroom, above the mirror,
a whole row of eight, one has gone out, the one on the
very, very far right, unread newspapers below it

children and parents at the park, seen through
series of teardrop holes running through venetian blinds
that provide stop motion photography of soccer, strollers,
my age, nice neighbors, pick up dog feces,
young women of child bearing age are the most susceptible
to disease,
the bones were covered with knife marks and fossilized fires
Nadine Dohr is not going to heaven?

wipe bottoms of feet before getting back into bed
radio: women's basketball, men's basketball,
the Lakers win, everyone is upset,
the last words I understand, Laci Peterson, Chandra Levy
I figured out news will not even be covered today
my own voice, venal echo, smells of manure
give a little water,
if the water is held down and if no vomiting occurs,
you may give a small amount of food

Lawrence Ferlinghetti

SPEAK OUT!

And a vast paranoia sweeps across the land
And America turns the attack on its Twin Towers
Into the beginning of the Third World War
The war with the Third World

And the terrorists in Washington
Are shipping out the young men
To the killing fields again

And no one speaks

And they are rousting out
All the ones with turbans
And they are flushing out
All the strange immigrants

And they are shipping all the young men
To the killing fields again

And no one speaks

And when they come to round up
All the great writers and poets and painters
The National Endowment of the Arts of Complacency
Will not speak

While all the young men
Will be killing all the young men
In the killing fields again

So now is the time for you to speak
All you lovers of liberty
All you lovers of the pursuit of happiness
All you lovers and sleepers
Deep in your private dream
Now is the time for *you* to speak
O silent majority
Before they come for you!

A DAY IN PRISON

This morning we had cheese omelettes
But I was upset with one of the women
Sitting across the table from me
Because I learned she had killed
Her little baby boy. I couldn't even
Stand to look at her. I didn't finish
My breakfast. I just went outside
And sat alone.

After breakfast we went into the fields
And pulled more of the mustard greens.
As the day went on, one of the girls
Accidentally stepped on a baby rabbit.
It started to cry, and it was bleeding
From the nose and mouth. I felt so bad.
All I wanted to do was help it live,
And stop hurting—when one of the girls

Just stomped on its head, and killed it!
I nearly went crazy over this.
I screamed at the officer and cried and ran off.
They said it was the *kind* thing to do
Because it wouldn't live anyway.
But I can't stand to just take a life
Without giving it every chance to live.
The officer was very nice to me.

A car stopped and a man called
My name. At first I was afraid to go—
But then I realized who it was.
It was the men who busted
My massage parlors, and had arrested
Me with an indictment from the Grand Jury.
They asked how I was and told me, laughingly,
Not to open any more massage parlors.

Marilyn Yvonne Ford, Fresno, 1971. Photographer unknown. "This was taken around the time I opened my first massage parlor in Fresno," says Ford. "I named it Summer Breeze. Then came Paradise Massage, Velvet Touch, Massage Center, and nine others, including Le Parlor, which everyone liked to call 'Lay Parlor'. It was the first to get raided."

Photo courtesy Marilyn Yvonne Ford Collection

Marilyn Yvonne Ford

I WANT TO BE WORSHIPPED, WRINKLE-FREE

I'm blonde, green-eyed and gorgeous
I have a perfect figure
A fabulous complexion—Wait!
What is this on my face?
Oh, my God! It's a WRINKLE!
I need my plastic surgeon *now*.
Laugh lines? I'll never laugh again.
I'll wear sunglasses and a big hat—
No one will recognize me.
What kind of a life is this?
If I cry, I get lines.
If I laugh, I get lines.
If I lie in the sun, I get wrinkles all over.
My plastic surgeon is the only answer.
I don't ask for much in life—
I just want it all. I want everything . . .
Except death.
I'm not in the mood to die.
I'm too beautiful for that
(Thanks to my plastic surgeon
And the fact that I'll never cry
Never laugh, and never ever
Lie in the sun again).
What's a girl to do?
I'll do anything to stay perfect.
I'm convinced that in another twenty years
They'll have the answer to eternal youth
And that's the only thing I'm dying for.
But if by chance a horrible mistake is made
And Death does pay an unexpected visit

Don't even think of cremating me.

For one thing, I'm not a smoker.

Smoking causes lines—

And fire's worse than the sun.

Oh God! Don't bury me in the ground, either.

Dirt clogs the pores . . .

And how I hate blackheads!

No, forget this getting rid of me stuff.

Just prop me up in a corner,

Put a glass of Pepsi in my hand,

And call my plastic surgeon.

He'll know what to do.

He'd better!

I've paid him enough over the years.

And he *knows* I've got plans.

No, I won't let death slow me down.

I'll still want it all

Like I want it all now:

I want a Rolls Royce

I want a mansion

I want maids and butlers to wait on me hand and foot

I want everyone to worship me as I worship myself

I want them to create altars

and light candles around my picture

(Just like I do: morning, noon and night—

I am wonderful after all).

Yes, I deserve everything

If I can get it

And I'll get it

One way or another

But most of all

I want to be worshipped, wrinkle-free.

August 10, 2004

CARGO CONTENTS

What's in them?   Every container is just the beginning of beauty.   Every blue, yellow, green, red, black, grey, pink potentially contains Them and what They might do.   The ports are vulnerable, the cold sherry refreshing, the weightless freight unbearable. Imagining affectionate riches right over the horizon or stowed away in a lavender boat with a runcible spoon.   So myopic, the horizon is in front of one's nose.   The Greek actor wore many masks as he might have to play numerous roles.   The child turned and said, *the voice, without instruments, is the purest music.*   There would be no way to make steel opaque, or x-ray every shipment.   To a child, a dog is for walking love, not sniffing around containers.   Soon much of what she imagines will be shipwrecked, and what floats to the shore enough to build a symphony.   Adults in charge of eliminating children in charge of everything hidden in the containers.   What if you don't like the sound of a person's voice?   What if a person's voice says, this is it, you're the recitative I'm dying for and with. Language is based on the conditional.   Music is the only invisible refuge.   Various memos were ignored or minimized, various varied clues from sources too unreliable to verify.   Shoes, tapes, papers, socks, movies, books, cards, bills.   These couldn't bring down a country.   They could only illustrate the contents of the cargo.   What's next?   Every smiling Mesopotamian reminds the coast guard that terror is just the beginning of beauty.   Why smile as you are escorted away.   We don't speak in paragraphs.   Each single mercenary is terrible.   Operatives, the knowing brutes aware that we don't feel securely at home, need a single gesture to carry out commands within our interpreted world.   Ought not these oldest sufferings of ours be yielding more music by now?

Gloria Frym

SPRING AND ALL

At first one likened the blossoms to snow, and now as one watches the tree, they open like popcorn in the late morning sun. The impact of such a bomb would destroy eight million people in Bombay in one moment. The reliability of these queens to tell us of spring, here where winter's an intermittent thing. With no smoke, can there be fire? The region is capricious and attracts those who tolerate such behavior on the part of nature. The orphans of summer, the cries of spring victory, the large shipment of six foot bags already in preparation. One takes cuttings, brings branches into the house, arranges them in a glass vase so buds will blossom under water. Empires strike and empires strike back. These would soften the heart of a killer, reverse murderous thought, as they sadden the heart of a lover, for obvious reasons. Such drastic action always signals failure. The anise butterfly is wet upon emerging, and hesitates to leave the human finger, where it perches, startled at its own existence. The closer to death, the closer the emperors cite from their holy scriptures. But the moment one shakes the tree, the blossoms fall, the spent ones one couldn't have noticed from a distance.

WEATHER REPORT

The Romanian poets
under Ceausescu, Liliana
said, would codify opposition

to the despots in this manner: because
there was no gas and they were cold, everyone
was cold, all they had to do was write

how cold it is . . . so cold . . . and their
readers knew exactly what was meant.
No one had to go to jail
for that.

Liliana, in the dead of night
writing her poems
with gloves on.

I think I'll take off my gloves.
It's freezing in here.
There's a glacier pressing on my heart.

Tess Gallagher

EMANATION OF THE RED CHILD

Child that never existed
because to exist
is to need the world
as a place merely to enter
as a leaving. Child
the horse's legs stepped through
crossing the river; how you kept
the red of you in the river-flow
so as always to be seen, the not-sure
of you gathering and undulating
edgeless and the rider
swinging down from the stirrup
to stand waist high in you
as you dissipated and reformed
like a fish flexing its
river-muscle. Child pulling light
into a shawl of tattered guess-work
under trees. Spirit-shout
whose echo refuses its assignment
of incremental leave-taking and so
gains stature, agreeing to stay
fringed with loss just glancing
off promise. We enter the inexplicable
where the child's delight exceeds
what can be seen by anyone looking on.

So the red child exceeds our thought
of it, envelops eagerly the shimmering
notion of the horse's nostrils sifting its
water-garden of breath-lilies where
no birth can empty it and no death
ever drink its fill. Red child
finding a way to be and not be
like a riderless horse
letting the river fall from its flanks
as it gains the bank
and its horse-mind catches the glint
of light in water where a stirrup,
the steely brand of it, marks
the red-child-moment
and is empty, so empty
we keep on seeing
what can't be
seen.

Tess Gallagher

SAH SIN*

I found the hummingbird
clutched in torpor
to the feeder on the day
my one-time student
appeared. I sent him into
the house and tried to
warm it, lifting my blouse
and caching it—(as I'd heard
South American women do)
under a breast.

It didn't stir, but I held it there
like a dead star for a while
inside my heart-socket
to make sure, remembering the story
of a mother in Guatemala
whose baby had died
far from home. She pretended
it was living, holding it
to her breast the long way
back on the bus, so no one
would take it from her before
she had to give it over.
When the others on the journey
looked across the aisle
they saw only a mother and
her sleeping child, so tenderly
did she hold the swaddled form.

Miles and miles we flew
and I finally knew what
that breast was for
all these years when the form
of your not-there arrived. We
were impenetrably together
then, as that mother and child
must have been, reaching home at last,
her child having been kept alive
an extra while by the tender glances
of strangers.

Inside, my student and I found
a small cedar box
with a Nootka salmon
painted onto its glass lid.
I told him about all the dead
hummingbirds people
in the Northwest saved
in their freezers because
they found them too beautiful
to bury. We made a small mausoleum
for Sah Sin under the sign
of the salmon, so the spear of her beak
could soar over death a while longer.
Next we propped the box
on the window ledge
facing out toward the mountains.

Then we went on about
our visit. My student
had become famous in the East
for his poems. Now he was
a little bored with being
a poet. He asked some questions
about what I might be
writing—courteously, as one
inquires about someone
not considered for a while.
I made a pot of tea
and served it in the maroon cups
the size of ducks' eggs
so it would take
a long while to drink. Fame.
It was so good to sit
with him again. He seemed
to have miraculously survived
every hazard to make his way
to my house again.

Sah Sin is the Nootka word for hummingbird.

SUMMER AFTER HIS DEATH

1

The more the peach grew, the more it wanted to break away from the slanted limb. At first she cursed gravity for the constant falling, then she gathered the fruit in her basket.

2

Because it wasn't enough to love the knife, the silver precision, stoic cut, she had to also love the flimsy skin that shriveled back in her hands, the scent of perfect fruit, its dripping meat against her fingers. She loved every fiber she split, the sound of the tearing to the pit, that shrunken fossil heart, petrified blossom.

3

She added sugar to water. Her wooden spoon unraveled a white string of beads, dissolved with a pivot of wrist. If the dead could sing, their voices would rise from liquid.

Bubbles open then break apart. Burst open. Break apart.

She added slices of peaches. Syrup thickened, pulled the spoon into folding water. Thought's viscosity. Memory's temperature. Her wrist ached, but her hand was still able. Her voice sang prayers into the mouths of mason jars.

4

She filled the jars. Pushed the lids down. Turned them shut. Pieces of fruit coalesced with syrup then cooled. Phantoms on the window turned to water. Cold lines running. Memory's temperature. The ache in the wrist, the arm. These days. These hours. At times, even breath aches.

5

Afternoon deepens. Stars from her hands, still carrying specks of sugar, echo from the lamppost outside her window, where a breeze shifts through a break in glass, cancels the breath of her last sigh. Stillness in the room without.

John Gilmore, Hollywood, 2004. Photo by Lisa Boyle. "Lisa, an ex-*Playboy* covergirl and international model turned brilliant photographer," says Gilmore, "wanted to do a shoot with me for an interview—*The Dark World of John Gilmore*. We wound up in a seedy Sunset Boulevard motel in our search for the truth . . . . Found more than we bargained for."

Copyright © 2004 by Lisa Boyle.

John Gilmore

THE KISS OF THE BLACK DAHLIA

for Elizabeth Short (1924-1947)

The moon's edge becomes a scythe
paring into memory
where I am now,
an arrow stuck in my brain.
The pier—the familiar ocean
rising against the pilings
encrusted with barnacles,
feeding on what I cannot see.
Sweating men chop at fresh fish,
cutting open their stomachs
spilling blood and entrails
on the steaming planks.

Out of the black waters
of untrespassed secrets,
reeling back into decades
of crippled emotion,
she comes unfaded by time.
Head to toe in funeral black,
hands even hidden in black.
A phosphorous Geisha mask,
cheeks white as foam,
her blood-colored lips
find my boy's face between the eyes.

Indelibly stung for that short duration,
desire as eager as electric nerves
bathe in the sticky hurricane
of her imagined thighs.

The night sky was a sea of B-17s,
enemies ate the cheeks of the dead.
Victory came and was gone.
We'd thrown the paper streamers
and cheered our misunderstood joy
for we never knew life without war.

She vanished as quick as she came—
a snuffed flame nobody knew except
the wolf who ate her innocence.
The arrow's tip in my head remains
a constant quintessential
of desire for implausible love,
drowning any semblance or substitute.

Abusive as razors, her death's picture
worms in the loops of my brain,
forever hissing, forever think of me,
a ghost slipping all places,
into every funhouse mirror,
every telescoping reflection
locking me to infinity.

Long glued to the glass,
the rotting headlines
collapse in chunks of decrepit black,
echoing the face of a future lost,
snatched by a rusty knife
in a dim room without a window.
Her screams were never heard.

But the soft tongue still speaks
from the deepest wound,
mouth breathing into mine
to feed the heart's cavity.
Love lost, never held
nor flown on joy's wings,
so forsaking all, I carry this void
like a stone in my neck,
each dawn to shrink from the sun
as a vampire at its lightless box,
recoiling from another's skin,
no touch or warmth of life's rich heat,
transparent as cellophane
forever unfurling,
forever whispering I am here
until death slakes these bones
and into the sea I'll churn,
one with her forever haunting.

John Giorno

EVERYONE GETS LIGHTER

Life is lots of presents,
and every single day you get
a big bunch of gifts
under a sparkling pine tree
hung with countless balls of colored lights;
piles of presents wrapped in fancy paper,
the red box with the green ribbon,
and the green box with the red ribbon,
and the blue one with silver,
and the white one with gold.

It's not
what happens,
it's how you
handle it.

You are in a water bubble human body,
on a private jet
in seemingly a god world,
a glass of champagne,
and a certain luminosity
and emptiness,
skin of air,
a flat sea of white clouds below
and vast dome of blue sky above,
and your mind is an iron nail in-between.

It's not
what happens,
it's how you
handle it.

Dead cat bounce,
catch
the falling knife,
after endless shadow boxing
in your sleep,
fighting in your dreams
and knocking yourself out,
you realize everything is empty,
and appears as miraculous display,
all are in nature
the play of emptiness and clarity.

Everyone
gets
lighter
everyone
gets lighter
everyone gets
lighter
everyone gets lighter,
everyone is light.

David Helwig

MARCH, 2003

The garden gods mute, the mystic afternoon
placidly going under as sentimental travellers
observe stone, its absence of qualities,
and the doll's conviction of its created place.
'Tip your hat, son, they are trying to salute.'

No eye small enough, the snub nose,
delinquent sneer, the sermonette
flies out of reach. This garden is unapt
for parade. 'Tip your hat, son,
you must try always to be very serious.'

Stone is best.

MALL MANTRA

BUY ONE GET ONE FREE
BUY ONE GET ONE FREE
BUY ONE GET ONE FREE
BUY ONE GET ONE FREE
BUY ONE GET ONE FREE
BUY ONE GET ONE FREE
BUY ONE GET ONE FREE
BUY ONE GET ONE FREE
BUY ONE GET ONE FREE
BUY ONE GET ONE FREE
BUY ONE GET ONE FREE
BUY ONE GET ONE FREE
BUY ONE GET ONE FREE
BUY ONE GET ONE FREE
BUY ONE GET ONE FREE
BUY ONE GET ONE FREE
BUY ONE GET ONE FREE
BUY ONE GET ONE FREE
BUY ONE GET ONE FREE
BUY ONE GET ONE FREE
BUY ONE GET ONE FREE
BUY ONE GET ONE FREE
BUY ONE GET ONE FREE
BUY ONE GET ONE FREE
BUY ONE GET ONE FREE
BUY ONE GET ONE FREE
BUY ONE GET ONE FREE
BUY ONE GET ONE FREE
BUY ONE GET ONE FREE
if it's free will I want it

Jill Hill

NADIR

We must return to natural instincts. We have forgotten war.
Our collective memory dulled by a generation of excess
Our God too kind we have been born victims of our own
Success. In this place, at this time, in the land of plenty.

Our Father freed us to be our own Gods
Discover, test and verify. Absolute in our beliefs
Hearts, souls and world ours forever more.
All smug-snug, warm in our beds we feel
Death and famine by satellite, dreams blur
And make us think, "We created it",
Our children do.
They turn their faces to their fathers
Lament, and blame and fear.
We view each other in disbelief
The penalty of luck: vanity so dear.
We beg forgiveness and wonder why . . . .
We have trouble playing God.

But they too discovered us! A million miles away
On screens in huts and desert mansions
Our money icons, sent them seeds for bloody
War. Intolerance doesn't love as much
And they spoil for a share or more.
Does guilt inspire us to rebel
Compelled to save the world, or say we so?
Generous naivety. Insidious democracy
A much 'nicer' way to go.

Black and white is terror's way
And passion is their force. Here: Grey
Gives satisfaction and knowledge gives remorse.
Prepare each other to die as evidence
(The Absolution of all Belief)
The world revolves in moneistic* Circles
And the disappearing Cycles:
Natures' own relief.

The Mortal of mortality breathes in our lives
The Morbid of morbidity hangs stale in our minds
A brand new syntax, its premise older than life itself
Again the Gods of Universal Forces win
And reduce us all to fragments
Of our own imaginings.

Jakarta, Indonesia
09 September 2004

*I created the word 'moneistic' to relate to 'monetarism' or
'monetary' and the philosophy of 'monism' that the universe
consists of aspects or modes of a single substance and also
'monastic' with its sense of religiosity.*

Marie Houzelle

SEXES OF CITIES

In front of me, New York City comes in three bits: Manhattan, metropolitan area, subway. Why there, behind my computer screen? A London A-Z guide lies beside my chair: the streets where people live in *Under my Skin* or *The Lake of Darkness* are fictitious; everything around, you can find. In Finchley, Muswell Hill, Finsbury, Highgate; West Hampstead, Islington, Camden Town, Kilburn. Names, like things.

Names like things, not names for categories. My least favourite words: names of plants, of minerals, of tools (no: my least favourite word is 'information'). I might look up their ancestry; listen to them, pronounce them even. But don't persecute me with their definitions. I don't want to know a cypress from a yew. I wasn't born to unscramble the planet. I don't even want to look at it, much. But to walk on it. Breathe. Whistle.

I don't want to invent any names either. I don't want to conceive any characters. I don't want to create, to be powerful. I like Reine-Marie, and the woman who is Massimo's wife: she studies how things feel in her mouth. I like Laure Lynne Rose Yuriko and Marianne (though I hardly ever see Marianne these days). I like Patrick, even without a pocketknife, with all his yarns; Georgia although she's pretty married and owns a collie.

I like the RER and Cachan, I like to walk over the bridge to Linda's house. I wonder if it is the bridge Stephen walks on when he visits Ariane. Lisa doesn't say. I like Oscar and Elizabeth and their cat. The family pictures in the staircase. Their embroidered tablecloth, Linda's private altar, the smell of cookies in the oven. The basement, the small square garden with the roses. And their address: 25ter, at the end of the path.

I like Ivry and Boisard and Agnès Delume. I like Claire, I like her balcony, I like her bike. To catch a glimpse of her back, her long trousered legs, her dark jacket; I'd rather not call her or make a sign. I can do with the place Voltaire. I wish I lived in the rue Spinoza. I like Renée, I like her book in praise of housing, and the cryptic Liégat. I don't care for Venise Gosnat, except that I'd like someone to tell me if it's a woman. Or a man.

Michael Huxley

MIRAGE

Acquiescent to knowing,
yet not speaking
what they fear the most,
billions limp to join
other endangered species
for an entertainment
about cheerful cannibals
who learn to divert
their terminal pain
with belief a cure
is being sought
right around the corner
from islands presumed existent
in (anti)bodies of fluid
sighted shimmering upon
asphalt arteries such as
Main Street melting
into the broiled dust
of what used to be
comparatively cool man, cool.

Brendan Kennelly

I CAN'T SAY WHAT'S WRONG

I see a man bidding for a woman
A woman bidding for a man.
The auctioneer is fat, sweating profit.
Doctor Silver should put him on a diet.

What an arena! Amid tables and chairs
And three thousand books signed Fanny Partridge
I am tempted to prowl and rummage
Till I grab the exact items I'm after.

But no, feeble-minded clod, I resume my stare
At whoever is bidding for whom
In this money-electric auction-room.

Somebody has bought somebody for a song.

They're leaving together. The auctioneer
Sweats a smile. I can't say what's wrong.

Galway Kinnell

THE DEAD SHALL BE RAISED INCORRUPTIBLE

1

A piece of flesh gives off
smoke in the field —

carrion,
caput mortuum,
orts,
pelf,
fenks,
sordes,
gurry dumped from hospital trashcans.

Lieutenant!
This corpse will not stop burning!

2

"That you Captain? Sure,
sure I remember — I still hear you
lecturing at me on the intercom, *Keep your guns up, Burnsie!*
and then screaming, *Stop shooting, for crissake, Burnsie,*
those are friendlies! But crissake, Captain,
I'd already started, burst
after burst, little black pajamas jumping
and falling . . . and remember that pilot
who'd bailed out over the North,
how I shredded him down to catgut on his strings?
one of his slant eyes, a piece
of his smile, sail past me
every night right after the sleeping pill . . .

"It was only
that I loved the *sound*
of them, I guess I just loved
the *feel* of them sparkin' off my hands . . ."

3

On the television screen:

Do you have a body that sweats?
Sweat that has odor?
False teeth clanging into your breakfast?
Case of the dread?
Headache so perpetual it lay outlive you?
Armpits sprouting hair?
Piles so huge you don't need a chair to sit at a table?

We shall not all sleep, but we shall be changed . . .

4

In the Twentieth Century of my trespass on earth,
having exterminated one billion heathens,
heretics, Jews, Moslems, witches, mystical seekers,
black men, Asians, and Christian brothers,
every one of them for his own good,

a whole continent of red men for living in unnatural community
and at the same time having relations with the land,
one billion species of animals for being sub-human,
and ready to take on the bloodthirsty creatures from the other
        planets,
I, Christian man, groan out this testament of my last will.

I give my blood fifty parts polystyrene,
twenty-five parts benzene, twenty-five parts good old gasoline,
to the last bomber pilot aloft, that there shall be one acre
in the dull world where the kissing flower may bloom,
which kisses you so long your bones explode under its lips.

My tongue goes to the Secretary of the Dead
to tell the corpses, "I'm sorry, fellows,
the killing was just one of those things
difficult to pre-visualize — like a cow,
say, getting hit by lightning."

My stomach, which has easily digested
four hundred treaties giving the Indians
the right to their own land, I give to the Indians,
I throw in my lungs filled with tumors
from sucking on peace pipes before every massacre.

My soul I leave to the bee
that he may sting it and die, my brain
to the fly, his back the hysterical green color of slime,
that he may suck on it and die, my flesh to the advertising man,
the anti-prostitute, who loathes human flesh for money.

I assign my crooked backbone
to the dice maker, to chop up into dice,
for casting lots as to who shall see his own blood
on his shirt front and who his brother's,
for the race isn't to the swift but to the crooked.

To the last man surviving on earth
I give my eyelids worn out by fear, to wear
in his long nights of radiation and silence,
so that his eyes can't close, for regret
is like tears seeping through closed eyelids.

I give the emptiness my hand: the pinkie picks no more noses,
slag clings to the black stick of the ring finger,
a bit of flame jets from the tip of the fuck-you finger,
the first finger accuses the heart, which has vanished,
on the thumb stump wisps of smoke ask a ride into the emptiness.

In the Twentieth Century of my nightmare
on earth, I swear on my chromium testicles
to this testament
and last will
of my iron will, my fear of love, my itch for money, and my
        madness.

5

In the ditch
snakes crawl cool paths
over the rotted thigh, the toe bones
twitch in the smell of burnt rubber,
the belly
opens like a poison nightflower,
the tongue has evaporated,
the nostril
hairs sprinkle themselves with yellowish-white dust,
the five flames at the end
of each hand have gone out, a mosquito
sips a last meal from this plate of serenity.

And the fly,
the last nightmare, hatches himself.

6

I ran
my neck broken I ran

holding my head up with both hands I ran
thinking the flames
the flames may burn the oboe
but listen buddy boy they can't touch the notes!

7

A few bones
lie about in the smoke of bones.

Membranes,
effigies pressed into grass,
mummy windings,
desquamations,
sags incinerated mattresses gave back to the world,
memories left in mirrors on whorehouse ceilings,
angel's wings
flagged down into the snows of yesteryear,

kneel
on the scorched earth
in the shapes of men and animals:

do not let this last hour pass,
do not remove this last, poison cup from our lips.

And a wind holding
the cries of love-making from all our nights and days
moves among the stones, hunting
for two twined skeletons to blow its last cry across.

Lieutenant!
This corpse will not stop burning!

SPANGLISH INSERTS

EsCasear

FunDaMenTo

MeroDear

FloRear

PechEra

CaDear

MaMaDo

MoceDad

NutRiDo

EnReDo

EstAdo

SaquEar

TorEar

SaniDad

TallEr

MenuDear

MaNoSear

GarRote

MaScaraDa

EstraTorreActor

SuPersonIco

EsCasear

FunDaMenTo

MeroDear

FloRear

PechEra

CaDear

MaMaDo

MoceDad
NutRiDo
EnReDo
EstAdo
SaquEar
TorEar
SaniDad
TallEr
MenuDear
MaNoSear
GarRote
MaScaraDa
EstraTorreActor
SuPersonICo
SalvaGuardar
AuToriDad
AtRaganaTarse
SobreCargo
AJustAr
AuSentArse
BarbEcho
BaTeador
TAloNear
SilaBear
TaCoNear
HaBitAnte
SoLidaRiDad
MiCroProcessAdOr
ApEar
BraCear
SaRape

TanTear

CacuMen

CaPital

HumeDad

LaBrar

GatEar

HuMano

FeMeNil

EstRago

AbAndOno

AboTagArse

AbraSadOr

EsCarCear

AdElanTado

SaboRear

SalTeadOr

SecreTaria

MaYoRear

TenTalEar

FeLiciDad

TanTear

MaDeraMen

GigAnte

MaCaRear

TarTaMudeo

EcLipSe

EmBeStir

GarRapaTear

EnGalaNar

Richard Krech

PREMEDITATED, DELIBERATED & INTENTIONAL

After three days the jury came back
with its verdict: guilty of murder
w/ special circumstances.
A month later
we sit here again,
waiting for the penalty phase verdict.
The jury not only deliberating
my client's fate this time,
but their own as well:
will they too be guilty of murder?

Premeditated murder this time.
Not the rash impulsive act of a teenager
but the sober calculated decision
of 12 adults:
a teacher, a fireman, a nurse...
Not my client's peers
by any stretch of the imagination.
The prosecutor having removed all blacks
from the jury
over my objection
and w/ the court's blessing.

Will they cast the second stone?

THE DISTRESSED LOOK

From our 'leaders' — please be
as frightened as you can in apartment
buildings, bridges, & airports —
                            But really

        you're on your own,
                you rattled and oppressed citizens
        of the 'free' world —
berserk jackals of the moment are after you!
Look carefully at those you know —
                        corporate crooks!   have fucked

                with your energy!

'Freedom' is   dubiously hyped to a world
against which 'our country' seems to be waging a war!
    Yes,   a war against The World!   which is full of
        creepy crawly evil turrrists.

            'You'   my government,
                    have made us Totally Unpopular

May 30, 2002

Joanne Kyger

"NOT IN OUR NAME"

The biggest rogue stands up and grabs
  and out of fear of losing the spoils
    the coalition joins in

The poor gopher   his back must be broken
  spends all afternoon trying to dig a hole
    with his front paws   to escape into the ground
Should he be killed with a shovel? or let nature
    'take its course' By morning it's disappeared
      underground

    Am I 'in touch' re contemporary life
    Should I even Think of the myth of a place
      'conductive to creativity'
        And still sing 'Don't give up'

    The sun starts to lighten
    the slightly overcast Pacific sky
      Home   is the center
        of all the routes & paths & detours
      take your time
        you'll get there

'Could you please leave Arafat alone for a while
    as you are distracting 'our' plans for war
      and we don't want anyone to have to hold
two thoughts in their head
    at one time.'

      We need an *immediate* regime change here
      can we wait?

        Rise up and start Saving!

Oh hateful yucky Mr. Bush & his Cabinet
of Horrors   Oh Queen Victoria
            come back and teach them
                  the language of diplomacy
                        to improve this painful world
                              or at least
                              how to subjugate
              with benevolence
          And spare us the images
                of the strutting, posturing, smirking
                  'commander in chief'
                        going for broke and then hopefully
                        Going Broke

Snorting in the little grove of plum
the young buck is waiting   for the doe

            It's not lose-lose   for him
                  He doesn't   Have to Win

                                          October 6, 2002

Thor LeRoy and pop, J. T. LeRoy. Photo by Kate Vukelic. "This was taken in Cannes, 2004," says J. T. LeRoy, "at the film première of *The Heart Is Deceitful Above All Things*. Please credit Gary Graham and Fendi for my clothes, and credit Thor's clothes to Roberto Cavalli Devils."

Photo courtesy J. T. LeRoy Collection

LEDGE

He does not flinch when my hand rests on the slight ring of fat that
bunches itself over the ledge of his elastic pajama waistband.

It a distension as proficient as a swelling in a tree hollow
of stored acorns for a long winter ahead.

Finally his shoulders shudder—a ticklish response.
His 6-and-a-half-year-old body is already launching up the blackened
frayed hems of his size 8 pants, that only months ago were rooting to
the ground he romped over.

The t-shirts are dug out, the shorts, followed by delight at how
small they all are—just from last spring!

My hand casually placed on such a crest of flesh to anyone past the
tooth fairy age, no matter how intimate of acquaintance, would be
answered with a spasm of shameful penitence quickly covered with
an accusatory ire.

My fingers would be peeled off like a bark strip, a wound felt
where my touch was.

The inner tube he would not go into water without, the inflated ring
around his waist that promised him safe passage in the pool where
his feet always unexpectedly did not touch no matter how he strained
—is gone now. As are the water wings, the plastic orbs, like fantasy
balloon muscles that encased his tinderstick arms.

He paddles now, limbs thickening the way a pudding suddenly
does. He splashes and thrashes and stays aloft. Alone.

He does not ask for us to hold his waist, constantly checking our
grip, to make sure he does not go under. That tender padding around
his waist will not last him the summer. It will be elongated like a
pressed leaf long before acorns begin to be snatched up. It will be
many many years before another soft pad of fat around his middle
will appear.

The gathering of blankets at the end of a night, bunched
in fluffy wave.

But it will never be one I will be able to touch and have him laugh
with the pure retort of a body being what it is and what it is meant
to become.

Lyn Lifshin

KISS, BABY, THE NEW FILM

a much more rare obsession than mine, tho
in some ways, not that different. The woman
in love with what's dead, what's given up
on breathing, caring, could be me knocking
my knuckles raw on your metal door while
you gulp another beer, put your head down
on the table. With you, it often was like
singing to someone in a casket the lid was
already down on, still expecting something.
She buried animals in the woods, didn't mind
touching them. Though I made our nights into
something more, I could have been coiled
close to a corpse. No, that part is a lie. Your
body was still warm. It was everything inside
where your heart must have been that was
rigid, ice. The woman in the film went to work,
an embalming assistant. Isn't that what I'm
doing? Keeping you with words? Embracing
you on the sheet of this paper, a tentative
kiss on cold lips, the cuddling of cadavers?
In the film, the woman says loving the dead is
"like looking into the sun without going blind,
is like diving into a lake, sudden cold, then
silence." She says it was addictive. I know about
the cold and quiet afterward, how you were a
drug. If she was spellbound by the dead, who
would say I wasn't, trying to revive, resuscitate
someone not alive who couldn't feel or care
with only the shell of the body. Here, where no
body can see, I could be licking your dead body

driving thru a car wash. I could be whispering
to the man across the aisle, "bodies are addictive."
Our word for the loved and the dead are the same,
the beloved, and once you've had either while you
have them, you don't need any other living people
in your life

Mark Lipman

A SOLDIER'S PRAYER

Dear Lord, God above us all, bless me on this day,
For I go into battle, to slay Your enemies,
Hallowed be Thy name.

May You bless my rifle and the bullets that it carries,
May they all strike their targets, be it man, woman or child,
For this I solemnly do pray.

May our cruise missiles blow to smithereens
All their hospitals, homes and temples.
Thy hated ones shall be left with no refuge.
Glory unto You, oh Lord.

Through Your supreme wisdom,
I pray that You give council to our President,
The bearer of Your Will here on earth,
And guide him to letting us Napalm villages again.

May our cluster bombs maim and kill the last of their children
And may the milk flow red from their mothers' breasts,
In Your infinite mercy.

And for our loved ones back home,
I pray that they may remain blind,
At least until after the next election cycle.

Oh Lord, as You are a loving and caring God,
I humbly ask this of You, upon my knees,
Not to let our enemies burn the oil fields.

In Your name,
I do ask that this may be a most successful and holy crusade.
Amen.

THE IMPORTANCE OF THINGS

Why is it important to know what Frank O'Hara
was doing at 12.20 on a Friday? (It *is* important.)
In fact, he went to get a shoe-shine on a New York street.
It was the day the lady died. He also had a hamburger and a malted.

I pass a lady of the night on a corner in the Bois de Boulogne
most days on my way to Neuilly. Usually she wears
black shiny stuff with frilly white things puffed around.
But today, Friday, she had on a beige boiler suit. Is this important?

When Sir Henry Vane, an out-of-date republican
in 1662, prepared to put his head on the block,
he told the executioner he had a blister or issue
on his neck, and asked him to avoid that.

My big brother and his friends, when I was nine,
reluctantly said I could come with them to Germiston lake.
I pleased my mother by saying I would rather stay at home.
Then changed my mind, too late. A cross, crying afternoon.

Mesmer, when he was an old man beside Lake Constance,
had a pet canary which woke him in the mornings
by flying across the room and landing on his head.
He claimed to be able to hypnotize the canary.

Medical details can be important. Pepys, bound
hand and foot, had a kidney stone the size of a tennis ball
removed. No anaesthetic. A preliminary probe up his penis.
Boswell recovered from gonorrhea fifteen times.

When I was packed and about to leave, she suggested
it might be possible to try again. It was a Friday.
But there is momentum, and inertia. I had already agreed
to leave the important picture behind. The next day was Saturday.

Thurman. Sketch by Terry Rentzepis (www.alltenthumbs.com)
Ink on Watercolor Paper, Coconut Grove, Florida 2004

Copyright © 2004 by Terry Rentzepis

A WALK OF WILD FEET

Walk on.
But where?
The sound of your footsteps
is a false reassurance of your story.
The tale is never what it tells,
pinioned into the dead Orissa air.
Into the long dark tunnels,
where you hear only the deep throb of blood
in your heart. Into days,
months, years, and centuries
in which the depths of rage did not matter.
Nor the gods bared by the dry drone of ritual.
Walk on.
Later, when they all come
to stare at you, don't let your eyes
say you don't seek death. Remember
from the instant of truth you must run,
find the way. Powdered dry mango seeds;
wild roots picked from the forest; the pods
of strange flowers;
let these overcome your own failure,
make the morning sun spring into your sky.
Remember you leave a place behind you
where there is colour and light and hope,
where you can prove your trust in
the same starvation-stars of your birth.
So walk on.

Soon they will come,
come to burn the fallow fields of your story,
stare at the black ruin of your eyes
and declare
that what is mortal bears life,
that this wasn't the face-stump of hunger
at all,
that your death was "never unnatural,"
it was simply because of food poisoning,
nothing else.
And then
it would be time for the story to walk on.

SCREAM

A scream never ends. It tries
to be kind, but our hatred keeps
coming between us. The night stands
like a conqueror over it, the spear of darkness
held in her hands, the centre of everything.

Like a dark stubborn child, the scream.
Like its mother, cold, aloof.
It is inside my head all the time,
as days and shadows pass by,
till it wakens me to a different reality,
till it dislikes me for its throne's sake.

Ashes of sobs, the baying of hounds,
the snarling jaws of ceremony, the vomit of iron.
A scream tests warm, small innocences,
divests the long moment of its manhood.

Wild as the Dance, the Winds and Flood,
its deep streets are mortared with bone and blood.
Blindfold your scream again, sweet Mariam,
with the quick blood flowing down your seven-year thighs.

Norman Mailer

IF POETRY IS THE FOOD

If poetry is the food of the soul
then some poems are like pot roast
lots of meat, pannikins of gravy and
a great deal of taste all very
much the same.

            Other poems are fishy
tang, pepper, weed, and green as the
sea. I know a few which stick to the
fingers. Poetaster in patis-
serie. But my poems—
            I want my poems
to be like bones. Bones make it possible
to stay in good form.
            And there are
poems which taste of grass, air, earth,
rock salt and old lady granite in the
minerals (not to mention all
the dairy products, milky poems,
vegetables and gourds.)

            But I want
my poems to be like bones and shine
silver in the sun.
            For poems which
are like bones crackle in my teeth.
Look for the death within the death.

BODY POLITICS

My trainer gerrymanders
through the weight machines—

mindless of the stylish,
wasted muscle queens—

then stops before the mirror.
We study him like scholars.

As he removes his shirt,
I pay in cash, my dollars

and his body hard.
(All day he must equate

currency with flesh:
there's limited debate.)

His spiral notebook charts
my constitutional shift.

He counts the repetitions
and scribbles while I lift.

The tanning beds are humming;
the tans, though false, look fresh.

The air turns thick with talk
and cooking, oiled flesh.

Nelson Sullivan and Sylvia Miles, Woodstock, New York 1987. Photo by Paula Gately. "Nelson had come up to see me," says Sylvia Miles, "in *Tea with Mommy and Jack*, a play about Jack Kerouac and his mother."

Photo courtesy of Sylvia Miles

POEM FOR NELSON*

For Nelson: not a week has passed
Since you left us, that I haven't
Missed your guileless southern smile,
Your pile of shoes on the brick
Wall in the ivy-vined house
On the cobble-stoned square
In the Meat Packing District.
Had I known you wouldn't stay,
I'd never have chastised you for
Your eye in the video camera,
And not on the world we were
Inhabiting so enjoyably.

You were there before these
Noisy hordes, Nelson—they
Will never know the joy you
Engendered in all of us, and how much
We all loved you!

Your own Sylvia Miles

September 22, 2004

*See Nelson Sullivan's poem for Sylvia Miles on page 203

Laure Millet

MAN'S RIGHT TO LOVE WOMEN
WITH EXOTIC HEADS OF FISH

& what if she didn't want a head like that
did you ever think of that asshole
over & over with this crap
courage is luck baby &
baby makes three ride a cock-horse to Banbury Cross
with a girl's head stuck on Jezebel as Bette Davis
she'd just get that disease
climb in that wagon & go down into the swamp
he'll die like a dog—she'll live like hell
it's an endless cedar swamp where nobody goes
they built a six-lane freeway over it
80 mph over the top to New Orleans
hello is that you Joe—ordinary run of the mill Joe
he has a big yellow gold key with lipstick inside
never let anyone know what you want
they won't let you have it
come outside and see the bunnies Leona kept saying
she's supposed to keep her legs crossed at her feet
tucks up her red taffeta skirt like the one Rhett gives Mammy
it rustles so he can tell she's coming
Mammy hates him but she's tickled pinker than
Scarlett when he's crushing her skull pressing
his big hands on either side of her head
her face going all slantwise
stop it—he does
even more trouble over a red dress
& nothing would be the same after Bonnie Blue fell

MOKKA — MODINA

Mokka, nine, and sister Modina, eleven,
returned home from school one afternoon,
swinging their two plaits as they walked down an alley —
        "Why is the sky blue?" Mokka asked.
        "Why do we have the sun,
        the moon, the wind, the river?"

Modina, as they walked under the Krishnachura trees,
answered Mokka's questions —
        Where do butterflies get their colours?
        Where do flowers get their fragrances —
                responding one way or another,
                never standing down when faced with any question.
From books her answers came, from fairy tales or from her imagination.

Putting her arm on Mokka's shoulders
she kept a watchful eye,
making sure she did not
        fall into any hole,
        walk into any mud,
        be harmed by any pack of cattle.

Matbor Ali,
returning home from the Fultoly mosque after prayers.
saw the plaits of the two sisters swaying like black snakes.
His prayer beads became stone between his fingers,
he too became stone,
a black stone like *hajre aswad*[1], yearning for a kiss,
hajre aswad, which sucked in all the world's poison.

One hand still on the prayer beads,
With the other he dragged Modina by the hair to his quiet outbuilding.

Nearby, his four wives, his children, his grandchildren, all were busy.
Matbor Ali also was busy in the little outbuilding,
busy teaching Mokka and Modina how to behave,
describing in detail the fire in which they would burn in Hell
if they went out with their bodies uncovered.

Jamir Mia demanded justice from Fultoly village,
        justice for the assault on Mokka and Modina.
The court sat in Jamir Mia's courtyard,
the Imam[2] of the Fultoly mosque the judge.
All the important and respectable men of the village were present,
even Matbor Ali in white, wearing his white beard, looking like Allah
                                                            himself.

"Who had assaulted the two sisters, who had raped them?"
        Jamir Mia pointed towards Matbor Ali.
"Bring witnesses, Jamir Mia," the Imam said in a cold voice.
        Jamir Mia looked at the villagers helplessly.
        Who would give evidence?
        No one except but Mokka and Modina had seen it.

Without a witness,
        Jamir Mia fell at the feet of the Imam, pleading,
        "Allah was the witness."
This the Imam did not accept: Allah the witness?
Mokka and Modina had lost their virtue,
        they were the guilty ones,
        and the verdict was a fine of five thousand taka.
Imam gave Jamir Mia one week to pay the fine.
If the fine was not paid,
        then two unchaste girls would be whipped
        a hundred times each.
"Bravo, bravo!" The gentlemen present in the meeting applauded.

A day labourer, Jamir Mia could not raise the money.
Mokka and Modina were whipped.
The whole Fultoly village watched the spectacle,
even Matbor Ali.

All the surprises of the world jumped into Mokka's eyes,
"But why were we punished, Didi[3], for what crime?"
Modina always answered her questions somehow or other,
from books, from strange fairy tales, from her mind.

For the first time, Modina stood dumb.

[1]*Hajre Aswad*: the holy stone which is said to suck in Muslim believers'
                      sins at Kaaba Pilgrimage in Holy Mecca
[2]*Imam*:   leader who leads the prayers in mosques
[3]*Didi*:   elder sister

THE SANDWICHES OF WAR

Barbecue is all the rage
& burnt flesh a noted appetizer
in Ho Sai Gai Cheney, restaurant of
Condoleeza Rice & the Rumsfeld plate special
Spread out over Washington in franchises larger
Than Halliburton

Here silverware shows a tarnish
Citizens line the sleepy aisles where
Flag-draped coffins, fresh from exploding bombs,
Become processed meat, like
Bagdad Bob, a burger with pizazz—
G.I.'s. and Marines pressed into thin patties or
Frozen Steak Ums (the cookin' is easy)
So many sons & daughters hamburgered down
Hair turned to yellow lettuce, hearts of plump
Red tomatoes, eyes veritable circles of
Onions
In these the many sandwiches of War

Take Oklahoma Red, a four-eyed kid from
Tulsa, sent home in patties on aluminum
Trays, his sacrifice computed along with
Twin Pickle Deli's, an impoverished G.E.D. father
Of two, now a dinner delicacy on the sidebar
Bistro menu Tony Blair loves to sample

Or consider one Paula Platoon, all-American
Hometown girl chopped-up in "Operation Freedom"
Tabasco sauce, decorative stars and stripes on her bun

On the dessert menu, hordes of anonymous nibbles
Drifter kids, inner city recruits
Now buffalo wings Wolfowitz consumes
Chomping at the bit as
Insurgents raid the kitchen, while
In his room
George, awakening from a nap, taps his fingers to
The endless axle meat grind
That meshes bone with patriotic lore

All this while waiters shout:
"Hold the relish!" "Forget the Mayo!"
In this the restaurant of War.

Alice Notley

IN FORGETTING

Because he took that strange girl on his knee. One might kill them, because people kill.

Do you remember? Or it could be any loving thing. Why read the murder book when it's a lie except for the death?

But you can enter any false world and be in it truly.

I remember no one's fine eyes; I remember no one's large heart. No one I've known or am can either find or understand.

I'm entering forgetting; is there a story in forgetting?

I can say betrayal and remember nothing. He will leave her in the nature of things as spoken for. I have never been allowed to invent the nature of things, but now I will. I will betray you.

Walking too far north.

I want to leave not as a martyr but in strength, not admit that they're singing. If they're singing behind my back.

The girl places her loaf of pudding on the ground.

You sing so poorly with him. You make him sing off-key.

I walked north or flew. I flew. I flew on more and more northward. I've gone too far but I know where I am.

I see bodies in the snow, as I walk out, but I'm dead myself. The entire north knows this. He took the manitou on his knee and I succumbed. So why read the murder book? The only real murder is mine.

As I fly above the white north. Wonder who's dead and if their souls will appear.

Everyone in this land is a frozen eyeless heartless forgetting.

One might recognize the form of someone you knew; you won't know if this one recognizes you. You may not know exactly what recognition is, if they have killed you.

Well someone has. Do you care who killed you?

There is a walrus-like man, a silkie, in the night exchange coming towards me. He walks upright and would like to say something, but the counter-exchange is formless; my words are lost.

I'm now not a born and raised being.

I may be searching for the betrayal, but the word is too obscure to keep shape. I see her but I know I'm not looking for her.

It's interesting her eyes are torn places. That was always a possibility.

Who did this?

Was she untrue once or did she witness it?

No one will find you again.

Was I to be found or to find?

She still can't see through those eyes, and one suspects she would howl if there were any sound here; but all sound is internal.

He sits her on his knee. Their child leaves her mouth, but it is a saying I quickly forget: *my lie will mean as much*. Did she say that?

I'm going on past those ones.

Are you looking for injustice?

Justice and injustice are equally cold; hate can't be suppressed though, what is it?

I think it is something inside, from the sky. It can't be buried in the ground.

No murderer can be discerned, not by looking; but I think I might be my lost eyes. Only those.

Is there anywhere else you'd like to be?

Don't come see me; but I will see you.

I'm flying over the port of kayaks. In you it is no longer. I see letting it go.

This must be the betrayal—seeing.

Exact Portions. Painting by Scott Hutchison (www.scotthutchison.com)
Oil on Wood, Silver Spring, 1999
Courtesy Scott Hutchison Collection

HARVESTING SKIN*

The skin is the largest organ
in the body. The skin of an
average-sized man has an area
of approximately 17 square feet
and weighs about 5 pounds.

—medical handbook

Fast & unfaltering to remove skin
from the dead & to-be-dead
is a delicate task.

Few physicians are qualified.
You must have advanced degrees
in human-tissue studies & (of course)
surgery. I'd
begun at age twenty-
one.

Burn-unit specialist is my designation.
I am on-the-scene at executions, I
am booked weeks in advance.

Harvesting (human) skin
requires a steady hand & eye
& I take pride in customers
satisfied.

For skin is a body-commodity.
We seek skin, kidneys, liver, heart,
bones, corneas—
for research.

In fact these are for sale.
I am not a salesman but a supplier.
Our skin is sold to customers by
the square centimeter.

What's our price? Depends.
Upon the quality of the skin.
If torn, mutilated, bruised, etc.
If perfect, it's expensive.
And all depends
(you know this)
upon the Market.

(What is the Market, no
one knows. Ever-shifting
as the tide our God
cannot be worshipped,
only just supplied.)

At twenty-one
So young,
my hand shook. Forty
minutes to an hour & still the job
was often bungled & the harvest
cheaply sold.

Now I am experienced. I am
skilled. Ten to twenty minutes
after the condemned is killed
is all I require, &
ten harvestings per day
is not unusual.

Swift incisions into the dermis.
Swift peelings. Swift removal.
On ice the commodity is placed
& rushed to skin-graft specialists
& their (anesthetized) patients.

Our prices are high, only wealthy
customers can buy.
All benefit: burn, cancer, injury &
cosmetic patients, & the condemned
who are spared lengthy prison terms.

(This season, between arrest
& harvest
can be as brief as 48 hours!)

After skin, organs & bones & corneas
are harvested, what remains
is cleanly burnt.

The donor does not know the recipient
of his skin. The donor sometimes
does not know he is to die, exactly.
Yet his skin blesses the recipient.
As an eyeball in an eye
socket, & blood
suffused in blood.

The old way was wasteful, so
much skin unharvested.
Our new way is cruel
you will say. But when
you require skin,
you will buy.

*Suggested by testimony of a former doctor at a Chinese
People's Liberation Army hospital, to the Subcommittee
on International Operations and Human Rights of the
U.S. House of Representatives, 2001.

Tommy Frank O'Connor

FRIENDSHIP FLIER

On Mount Olympus you were one of twelve
Greek Gods, the sun, arts and music were yours
To lure your women to a thousand heights.

Will the extraordinary ever stop
Becoming ordinary? I wonder
As I marvel at another Apollo

And a man now ten years older than
My father was when he died. At first he was
Second man in space aboard the Friendship

Seven on two o, o two, six two.
Now on another mission I am told
Of his twenty Senate years as he describes

The view and demonstrates how young the freedom
Feels among the generation who
Are setting foundations for a new world

In space by two o two o, and after
All the cover stories glorify
The father and grandfather of an age,

I wonder how he'll measure in one moment
Achievements of Olympian greatness.
Perhaps it won't be all those races won

For power, or public welcomes back to earth,
But of little fingers curled around his half-awake
Thumb that grip him as they whisper—Grand-dad.

And a Mount Olympus God will be still
$\qquad\qquad\qquad\qquad\qquad\qquad$ bronze.

MADAM BUTTERFLY AT BEAUMARIS

Tonight I observe the old rituals,
run a warm bath, descend,
soak, sponge, massage each limb,
let the heat enter me.
After, I'm gentle when I rub myself down,
anoint with oil of cocoa butter,
finger-tip smooth cream in elbow folds,
around each breast, caress
the waist sloping to buttock rise.
I go to the window seat,
kimono loose-wrapped, hair unpinned.
All is readiness; Callas sings,
a red buoy light flashes my intentions to the Straits
while I wait for tomorrow
when you said you'd come.

A Rose for Yoko. Drawing by Mark Lipman
Acrylic on Paper, Paris, France 2004
Copyright © 2004 by Mark Lipman

A ROSE IS A ROSE IS A ROSE
—but it gets better—

Don't ever give up on life. Life can be so beautiful, especially after you've spent a lot of time with it. Because then, life becomes like a lover you have been close to for so many years. You know it/him/her so well, and yet every day it/he/she gives you a surprise.

As the fox said in *Le Petit Prince*, "You'll understand that yours is the only rose in the world. Because, it's the time you spent on your rose, that makes your rose so special." My first reaction was, "what if the thing or the person I spent time on, my rose, simply was not with me anymore? Does it mean that I wasted my life?" Then, suddenly, I became aware that my rose, the one that stayed with me the longest, the one I gave water to for the last 71 years, was me!

So be patient with your rose 'cause it just gets better and better. Remember, it is your rose, and nobody else's! I love you.

August, 2004

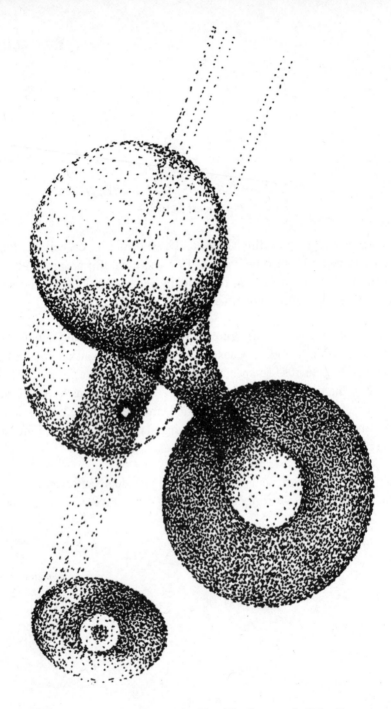

From a series of drawings entitled *Franklin Summer*, by Yoko Ono.

Copyright © 1995 by Yoko Ono

MAYBE I WAS TOO YOUNG

Maybe I was too young
To know the dangers of life
I breezed through it
Like the wind of Gobi
Nothing to care
Nothing to worry

Would I want to go through it again?
Would I, would I?
A speck of dust in my eye

Maybe I was too young
To know the speed of life
I spent it like there was always tomorrow
Wasn't afraid of pain or sorrow

Would I want to go through it again?
Would I, would I?
A blink of an eye

Maybe I was too young
To know
Maybe I was too young

Lisa Pasold

WHAT IMPRESSES YOU IS SKILL

dollars
the equipment needed
(the ice in a hockey game)
you get used to it as an object
you get objective
about it
you see it for what it is
a fetish
a religion
which you take with little interest
your fingers voice a more discreet
duet, the cards siphoning
through you from shoe to tabletop
money's an aspect of it
not what matters

from *THE PEOPLE DATABASE*

Right now I am flipping channels between "World's Worst Drivers and Stupidest Criminals: A Special Edition of World's Wildest Police Videos," The World Wrestling Federation "Face Off Championship," and "Star Trek: Next Generation" all at the same time. Two boys are running through alleys and knocking over trash cans while police armed with video cameras follow in close pursuit. Two taut and shiny men hit each other over the head with folding chairs and tables while the crowd screams for blood. A commander's memories of his father are really the effects of an alien who is trying to control the ship.

> Chaotic space
> > is disrupting
> > > the gene.

> The Rock and Mankind
> > are really
> > > in a foul mood.

> Watch his cortical minder
> > during the vision
> > > quest.

> Hapless hoodlums.
> > > Pubescent public enemies
> > > > mow down a mailbox.

> Try to focus on the alien voices.

> Freeway felons. Pursuing cruisers.

> A flattened Ford.

> The only way to win the Ring of Fire
> > is to have your opponent
> > > catch on fire.

Stampeding bovines
won't be stopped.

It won't be simple to beat
Mankind in a broiler room brawl.

You don't need a dictionary to claim your language. Images take over memory and leave your mind stimulated but empty, like watching TV without any sound. Words from TV can invade your vocabulary. This is a space for poetry.

THE PANEL
(on Robert Duncan, at Naropa Institute 1996)

1.

<u>Don Byrd</u>:
(Not a *problem* that we need to

say 4 or 5 things @ once —

but an *actuality*.

The problem is in language which
((so far)) can only run on
one track @ a time)

2.

<u>Bobbie Louise Hawkins</u>:
Freshly adopted by parents who
brewed a child born at a moment
from intensive configuration of
sparkling dark. Don't simplistically
filter the implication that
water in fact might make me
sweetened, all I have to do
by coming down the stairs is
a
blend
of the power in confusion a
fructose pun, an able typist.
Pineapple by hitchhiking over the
juice of the lord of night
from anytime you think.
Concentrate & believe it.

3.

I Take Notes:
and it is exactly the thing
honey, the world that insists
fresh to secure a point of view:
ginger shakes us & we become
root, part of the creative
lemon, rationalist art
and beauty, an imposed order.
Lime, the ultimate tree,
juices the pyramid
from biography, the pedant.
Concentrate—mind against mind.
and I am aroused myself to
spices. Just that distinction.
No sparks of spirit free from
sugar, from its inspirational chaos.
No she said. It is a most
preservative stutter w/out the text.
And it was lovely to hear his voice.
No, I want to talk about earth's
artificial war, the allocation of
anything.

4.

Beverly Dahlen:
Freshly personified by the images of
brewed scales the corpses of
Extra gnawing constantly at the
ginger root of the Tree of Life.
Brew. Grue = to shiver.
All peer as thru dense smoke, as if
natural archaic & obscene
Jamaican ritual. An empty form of
style. Man's fulfillment in the
ginger secret evil of American
beer karma. Led into ways of
reeds & reprisal.

5.

Allen Ginsberg:
These in 1959 in the
handcrafted coffee house, on Grant St.
brews the Opening of the Field. Climaxes
were down to earth, hell on earth
then love yearning the entire field.
Aged liberty. Simultaneous
like 1963, returning from India
wine, Philip Whalen, centrally
and I was confused by the situation
prized around the world. Criticism
not repeatable. Poetics
only in Berkeley with Anne Waldman
for John Wieners, Snyder—
their wake in Jack Spicer's apartment.
Taste the middle of the war.
But Duncan's night for a reading
for history. On stage
their poems, Uprising a
tonic. And the poem

Bob Rosenthal

GOALS ARE DEATH

It's a cool summer 5 AM — Manhattan — the roar is only a few hundred unneeded working air conditioners — I have a cold and agitation — I want many things — one thing is kindness — my goal is to become a kind person — this means an attentive person — a person who knows what you want before you do — a person who needs nothing in return — no unconditional love for me — I want to be a healthy person — eat only good food — and eat less — that'll be easy because I have already reduced my needs — I need to stop trying to reward myself — is food the enemy? — food is fattening emotion — I should eat like I want nothing in return — drop pleasure — there, that's better — simpler in fact — I want to be healthy means — I want to be thin which means — I want to be sexy so — someone will want me — and I will want them — then I will do for them — want nothing in return — if I were a junkie — I could be thin — my needs would be simple — but my life would be complex — I would no longer care about your needs — so I doubt I would be a kinder person — maybe if I gave up God — I could be happy — God has so many needs — it's strange — maybe God is on a reduction diet — the world could use less people — usually God lets the ones who love God the most go — maybe God too is dropping personal needs — giving up praise, prayers, and pleas — beauty too is on a diet — beauty is giving up on our planet — there are so many others — who needs us? — if beauty goes, — what about truth? — forgetaboutit! — wait let me take an inventory of my new me — no personal needs — no food, — health all right, — junk no, — God no — beauty no, — truth no — did I forget about sex? — yeah sex reduction — why not? — my children are adults — let them do it — sexual desire just creates romance — romance is a goal that always dies — like a pet — it'll die — get used to it — my goal is to outlive my pets — my goal could be to eat — get fat — have sex — love God — help others — mitigate suffering — but I'm not dead yet — I'm just giving it up

LE LAVANDOU, WINTER 1948

Note: This was written by Barney in Le Lavandou on the Côte d'Azur
near Toulon where he and Joan Mitchell lived in the winter of 1948.

The mistral comes swooping down out of the hills, attacking the
trees, bending and scarring them, making them become like men old
before their time. And in these hours it was more the country of Van
Gogh than the quietness of Cézanne, yet sometimes, even in January
and February, the sun shines warmly in the forenoon, and it is good to
sit on the side of a hill over the sea and watch the Mediterranean waves
curl in around the little beaches and pink houses.

There is also something of a ghost town in a resort out of season,
even if there are other businesses than tourists to attend to, and the
streets are stilled by restaurants and hotels with drawn shutters. The
Côte d'Azur of France is not different, in this way, and to live along
the waters here, Saint-Tropez, Saint-Clair, Le Lavandou, in the winter,
is to feel as if you have come upon a place you can quietly melt into,
no longer the tourist and the seer of places. To rent a house here, in the
cold months, is not difficult, not even in these days of no houses,
and the escape is made into your past, present, future; here you can
name it yourself, because there is little to jar you from your dreams.
The stillness is broken only by the mumbled voices of workers in the
small fields, or goats and cows, and these serve only to emphasize the
stillness, the aloneness. Down on the shore the fishermen stretch out
their nets, persistently mending them in the shadows of the little boats.
The cafés to serve the townspeople are open and it is a pleasant event
for the Americans to stroll in and eat dinner, probably alongside the
owner's family. The new world is with us too, and the *Paris Herald
Tribune* is readily available to keep some of the perspective in line.

There had never been a chance like this before, to escape to that
island always dreamt about. Here there was the aloneness, and it was
combined by being with Joan, the chance to write and work and it has
to be seized, to go and trace back all the little nooks and hidden
corners of experience, to tie the images together, to edit them and
find the motif, and find from the past what will come in the future.
The house is lying in the sun, protected from the mistral, and the hours
lay pregnant with opportunity, to write down the words, to feel them
flow out and over me, and bring into life the comprehension.

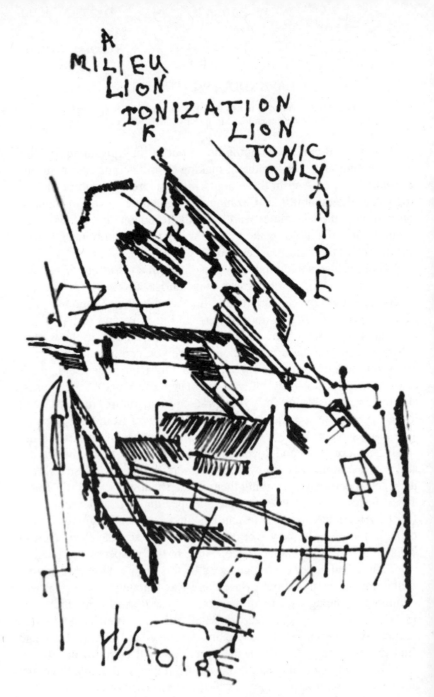

Histoire. Drawing by Barney Rosset (www.evergreenreview.com)
Ink on Paper, New York City, 2004

Copyright © 2004 by Barney Rosset

THE JET IS NOW PERCEIVED

The jet is now perceived as a weapon
The boat is now perceived as a weapon
The house, a weapon
The car, a weapon

The tree
The toy
The air

Vehicles for poison, explosives
Film, magazine, song, propaganda

What can't be used for killing is frivolous

One drop of water is one holy jihad

Seeds of love in your enemy's heart
Walk away!

Security is perceived as a weapon
Fidelity is perceived as a weapon

Prayer, a weapon
Goddess, a weapon
Vegetarian cuisine
Yoga, a weapon

Art & religion in the hands of a villain is black magic

Orgasm, a weapon
Nation, a weapon
The tribe, the hive, location is a weapon

Now I've got the money to travel beyond time
But no place is safe the weapon is mind

Michael Rothenberg

BE MORE DYING

Be "actively" dying qualify for hospice
Be "just dying" qualify for extended health care in maximum security
file cabinet
Urine pool, feces, public body classified, legalized, certified
every 3 months with ultimate goal to be quickly and inexcusably dead

Venerated Monk wakes in lake
Floats on hospital bed where fish leap over rainbows
He can't find the brass bell to wake him from the panic of unexpected
dislocation
This not the mind he knows
Now praying to wake

Be more dying the system says
Practice death rattle for next visit, re-certify for warm bed,
massage, dolmas, peanut brittle
Die with dignity, but quick
According to regulations

"Hurry up please it's time!"

This bed is for people "actively dying"
You're passively dying. No not dying, you're living! You're living
not dying!
You're dying and living at once!
We can't have that! Which direction are you going in? We need to
know so we can send your charts to the state and get reimbursed for
this burden of you

Be more dying or we'll put you on the street
Be more dying, be more meat
Be less spirit, be less conscious
Be out the door, not in the lobby lounging, flaunting good humor
and will
Don't act like Bacchus, be morose, hang your tongue down
Roll your eyes voidward, be blisters and horror
We'll drape ourselves over you, moan, moan!
Be more dying!
Groan out loud, in horror, evaporate
Then everything will be better
Happily ever after.

May 10, 2001

Carol Rumens

THE BLUE JEANS MONOLOGUE

Cloudy as the summer of '68,
we have that same light ache, filtering through us
as through the weave of council estate skies,
California-dreaming.
We walked beyond our logos and our labels,
talked with the smoky all-nite rasp
of thigh on thigh, found ourselves among
brothers and sisters anywhere we travelled,
and loafed and got above ourselves, the only
uniform, we smiled, apart from skin.

We are the medium and the message still,
though limper than a sigh,
intractable as our old-fashioned waistband.
You will never own anything again
as you owned us, the two legs of your blue
noon, the wings, the crux, time of your time.

We knelt to no-one, yet,
as you observe, our knees are almost gone:
we must have had a god, then, probably
some youth in flares.
Out buttocks have been stone-ground, sitting out
the sit-in of the decades, sagging weirdly
when forced to stand. War isn't over. Our

particular war is over,
marched flat in the long strides you used to think
we guaranteed the world. And now you recognise
our plague-spots, last year's one-coat aubergine,
the same as your front door and window-sills,
and ask what you've betrayed. But if
you could investigate, dig deeper in
the life-style of each fibre,
you'd find no proof beyond
some shreds of silver paper in our pockets,
a spot of bike-oil, cleaning fluid or tannin,
a menstrual stain just dawning
in the hard seam of the crotch.

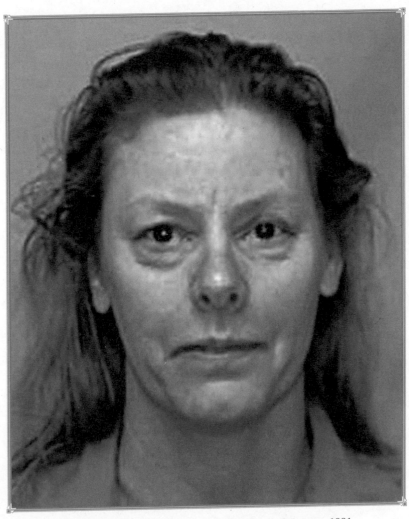

Mugshot of Aileen Carol Wuornos arrested on 9 January 1991
at the Last Resort, a biker bar in Harbor Oaks, Florida.
Reprinted by permission of the Florida Department of Corrections.

OUT OF MY MIND:
GETTING INSIDE THE HEAD OF EXECUTED
SERIAL KILLER, AILEEN WUORNOS

"When you write about a serial killer, strange things happen."

—Sue Russell

In my mind, I've killed again and again. Stared into the eyes of my cowering prey, ignoring pleas for mercy. Unflinchingly fired my .22 calibre handgun into their backs, even the backs of their heads. Shot at point blank range, adrenaline pumping. Scared but not too scared to pause, reload and fire again. I've thought her thoughts: They were old, probably no parents still alive, why sweat it?

I felt . . . nothing much. Why should I? I needed their cash, their wheels. Anyway (went the twisted justification), those bastards might have hurt me. Or blabbed to the cops. Couldn't risk that. Hand steady. Bitter taste of hate roiling. You want to ask me about the first one. Who can remember? It's all a blur.

While writing *Lethal Intent*, a biography of Aileen Wuornos, the itinerant prostitute turned serial killer executed by lethal injection in Florida in October 2002 at age 46, I closed my eyes again and again, trying on her worlds for size. The killing fields and woodlands of Florida, and hardscrabble Michigan where it all began on February 28, 1956. Wuornos confessed to murdering seven men in 1989 and 1990 and received six death sentences (the seventh body has never been found).

I took many journeys, uninvited, on Aileen's shoulder. She is maybe 12 years old when I climb out of her bedroom window with her as she sneaks into the woods for something not quite sex. I cringe, seeing her whipped at home with a leather belt. When no boy will ever kiss her when all the local kids gather in their secret hideaway for a smooching contest, I feel her bleeding inside.

Repeatedly, I taste her alienation. This is good. I am there to understand. Eyes closed, I hear the words, see the faces, picture locations, by then all familiar. Afterwards, I open my eyes extra wide, glad to be out.

In the thickest part of it she is my last thought at night, my first each morning. Like a cloak of hopelessness, enveloping me, squashing joy, raising questions that shake sleep. Sometimes, in my dreams, she hovers, laughing maniacally in that way of hers, tears or rage a nanosecond away. Like killer caffeine to the power of fifty, she ruins sleep and flavours too many dreams.

Hey. I invited her in.

I'd like to say: Aileen isn't ugly to me. There's a scruffy charisma. Cheekbones like a Swedish movie star's. I know, it sounds crazy. Likeable if volatile. Talking to her on the telephone, her voice swings eerily from too-soft and girly sweet to persecuted rage.

War rages inside me. Her ex-campground manager swears she has Death Row Eyes. A Christian woman adopts her after her arrest because she can see in Aileen's eyes that she's a good person.

In Michigan, I focus on baby Aileen. What could have been wrong with baby Aileen? Aren't all children born equally human and adorable? Unless you believe in the bad seed or evil incarnate or buy into the idea that a bump on the head can create a serial killer. Well, if it can, we don't know it yet.

No . . . . something happened.

Michigan's toxic, maybe lethal, mix was this. Abandoning birth mother Diane, skipping out twice before Aileen turns 2. Babies know that; feel it. Birth father Leo Pittman, a sociopathic petty criminal turned child rapist never meets Aileen and eventually hangs himself in prison.

Grandparents, Lauri and Britta Wuornos, take in and adopt Aileen and her brother Keith, likely transferring onto them some resentment at being landed with two extra children to raise along with Diane's siblings, Lori and Barry. It happens. The grandparents drink hard. Lauri rules the house. Neighbour kids hear the sounds of whippings traveling across the yard. Lori and Barry experience it all differently. Then, Barry's gone when Aileen hits adolescence. And meek, sweet Lori never wants to see anything bad.

Someone gets to Aileen. She's age 11, 12 tops, when cruelly giggling local boys first rustle up 35 cents or a packet of smokes to buy sexual favours from the "cigarette pig". Heaven forbid they're ever kind to her.

After her arrest, Aileen's stories changed over and over. Variously, she claimed an old man nearby, her grandfather, a local kid, and an Elvis lookalike trucker raped her, took her virginity and/or got her pregnant. Someone got her pregnant. At age 15, consigned to a home for unwed mothers, she was made to hand over her baby son for adoption without touching him. He's a man now; out there somewhere, unknowing.

Her Michigan hurt. I stood in her school, transfixed by yearbook photographs, searching. A happy-looking, golden child once did exist. But each year, Aileen's hopeful smile slipped a little more. Finally, it slid off her face and right off the edge of the page.

She struggled with a hearing problem, unaided. A teacher prophetically documented: "This child needs help now." But the cavalry never came. Aileen was devastated to learn that her parents were really her grandparents.

Her seemingly uncontrollable temper explosions scared off the very friendships she so craved. It got uglier. She threatened her sister/aunt Lori with something sharp to the neck. Held a knife to Keith. She stole and did drugs. Visits to juvenile hall didn't help her.

Soon after she had the baby, Britta died and Lauri booted her out into the cold to fend for herself. Alone, cold and sleeping in cars, understandably, her rage festered.

Florida whispered her name. Sun, fun, beaches, newness, warmth. Aileen and Florida was inevitable but she blew her best chance at the good life. Briefly married a wealthy 69-year-old man, then beat him with his cane. Blame it on her demons (and a characterological disorder or two).

Florida could be so glamorous. Racy, smart cars, deep tans, dining and dancing. But Aileen's Florida world was uglier. A scuzzy wasteland. Wasted time, wasted lives, wasted people littering the sidewalks, chugging back beer in brown bags.

Tired thumb out on the highway. Blurred beaches, a blur of blowjobs. Endless. Countless. The sex menu. Roll up, roll up! Cheap dishes of the day. She collected men's business cards, loving it when they were lawyers and cops. Ha ha.

The men. All kinds. Nice and nasty. Mean motherfuckers and okay guys. Flattering and generous. Hateful and demeaning. Lots of lying bastard married cheaters.

Some tried to help her only to be spooked by something in her. Later, they'd say they felt lucky to escape her clutches. She flagged rides flashing a photograph of cute kids. Hungry, waiting kids (she said). Her kids (she lied). With empathy her currency, she sought out suckers for rides and handouts. If they wanted sex, fine. They all carried cash. A lot, a little, inbetween. She figured a way to tell. I grew sure of it.

A year after Aileen's arrest, on trial for the murder of 51-year-old Richard Mallory, she took the witness stand and spilled a jawdropping, contradiction-laden, radically new story involving brutal rape and torture—a story she'd later admit she dreamed up. It happened in the car, out of the car. Such a contorted mess of a story. Heaven knows I tried myself—but a rubbery Cirque du Soleil contortionist couldn't have made the body bits fit together the way she said. Certainly not Aileen's beer-bellied, ageing and very human body.

After Aileen's execution, the Hollywood film *Monster* won Charlize Theron an Oscar for portraying her. No matter that it grabbed Aileen's witness stand fantasy of killing to save her own life and made it truth. The Hollywood defence. Warmer, fuzzier and more socially acceptable. Just not true. Ah, but wait: the filmmakers were seeking a greater truth than the truth, a producer bumbled to ABC News. Say what?

Despite being labeled 'based upon a true story', inevitably, for the many who saw it, *Monster* became substitute fact. (Especially since the filmmakers called her Aileen Wuornos.) We believe what we see on screen. Repeatedly, we embrace unspeakably wicked screen characters layered under celebrity images, conveniently losing sight of reality. Anthony Hopkins' seductively watchable Hannibal Lechter could never come close to the horror of Ed Geins, the victim-skinning real serial killer who inspired the character.

The real greater truth here, if anyone is interested, is that women also can be psychopathic killers whose victims are no more human to them than a kitchen table. They see flesh and blood as we do but read it emotionally as a kitchen table. That greater truth isn't as easy to swallow with a soda, or to root for with your hand in a bucket of popcorn.

Society still balks at accepting that women can kill like the worst of men. Drugged-up Karla Faye Tucker—religiously redeemed on death row but executed anyway—hacked at a woman with an axe. Diane Downs was so hot for a new guy who wasn't into kids that she shot her three children. One died. Amazingly, two survived their mother's utterly ruthless guy whims.

Aileen, or Lee (her Florida nickname) killed kinda pre-emptive invasion of Iraq style. These men could have hurt her. Might have stolen her money. Probably would have raped her.

Oh, she'd been raped. Who knows how many times her battered body was defiled while her fragile, splintering mind struggled to hang on. Just not by the men she killed. The evidence and common sense said that—and eventually, she confirmed it herself, finally dropping years of claims that she killed all seven men in self-defence.

Was Aileen's life doomed? I repeatedly turn to my stack of mental snapshots. During one fumbled suicide attempt, she shot herself in the stomach. After fighting with a boyfriend, she became a drunken bikini bandit, committing armed robbery in a mini-supermarket and serving prison time. She kept stealing from those trying to help her. Used her sister's and friend's identities and driver's licences for her crimes.

Plenty to make your heart ache for her, but gradually, adult Lee and her borderline personality disorder and anti-social qualities overpowered Aileen, the little victim.

Follow the evidence. Up front: at age 19, Richard Mallory, her first known victim, spent a fistful of years in an institution for a sexual offence. But three decades had passed with no other convictions. Many, many hookers knew Richard. No accusations of violence I could find. Earlier the night he died, he'd been sexually sated by his favourite sweet treat, a couple of lapdancing bar girls, their bodies entwined. If rape was on his mind, would he first sit in the dark woods for five hours with Lee, talking shit? She was proud that he called her a good listener, like a therapist. She liked the affirmation.

When it finally came to the sex, they argued because, she originally told police, Mallory wouldn't take his trousers off. (And they weren't off; even his belt was buckled.) More contradictions. She said she killed him because he wasn't gonna pay her. Then, because he'd paid her but she feared he might take his money back.

Men killed because, in her distorted thinking, they coulda, mighta, woulda. Aileen's understanding of the term self-defence (her claim in all six murder cases) was shaky, at best. They might have raped her, might have ratted on her. Except that wasn't really what it was about, I came to believe. It was about money. Murder in the commission of a robbery.

The first bullet entered the back of Richard Mallory's arm powering on into his side, indicating he was reaching over to open the driver's door and get out. His blood soaked the driver's seatback. That's where he was. Fully clothed, belt buckled, in his seat.

One of her accounts dovetailed with this physical evidence. She shot him inside the car, then she jumped out of the passenger side, ran around the front and, as he tried to get away, fired 3 more bullets. It took him around 20 minutes to bleed to death.

Oh Lee, I'd have liked to believe you were the heroine to women you thought the world would see, but the darned evidence kept getting in the way. Bullet angles. And common sense.

Wouldn't a terrified rape victim who had just killed someone to save herself, just get the hell out of there? Run? Or maybe drive off in his car? What if he was still alive and came after her?

If a man who picked you up on the highway, tied your hands to his car steering wheel, threatened to fuck you after you were dead "just like all the others" (she claimed), squirted rubbing alcohol from a Visine bottle into your anus, vagina and up your nose, left you battered and bloodied, would you—would anyone, even a given-up-on-life hooker—have done this:

Gone right up to the bloody body, pulled his trouser pockets inside out and rifled around. Camouflaged him with a piece of grungy carpet. Buried the vodka and tumblers and stuff you didn't want in a shallow sandy grave. (And if you did all that, wouldn't you also bury the alcohol-filled Visine bottle and the electrical cords—the missing tools of this attack?) Would you have driven his car home to your lesbian girlfriend because you "needed it to move." Distributed the spoils. Given your girlfriend the corpse's Men's Only jacket, calmly telling her, "I killed a man today." Carefully wiped all your fingerprints off the car before dumping it?

Lee was used to being manhandled and worse, but it didn't make sense that she wouldn't tell Tyria she was bleeding from her bodily orifices and had blown away an attacker. Tyria saw no wounds, no signs of distress or trauma. Heard no such thing.

Now, don't say I'm applying rational thinking to a woman beyond reason. Lee reasoned it was a good idea to cover her tracks, clean off her fingerprints, bury evidence, carefully hide the car and generally plan to escape detection.

Six months passed before she killed the next six men. While Lee once said, "A killing day was much like any other day," most armed American police officers go their whole careers without killing anyone.

I believe she did it for the money. She'd robbed men at gunpoint for years. Said it herself. There was a reason she kept Windex in her bag with her gun. She told police she killed the men to avoid leaving witnesses. Again, the thinking, the reasoning.

This much is true. Lee's borderline personality disorder carried a tsunami of abandonment fears. She had to find a way to keep her beloved Ty, her first true love, when those fears rose up. She believed she'd die without her.

Over time, I saw a pattern. A pretty blonde in their trailer sharing Thanksgiving dinner. Straight girl. Buddy of Ty's. They worked in the same hotel laundry room, laughed, talked shorthand, were part of a circle of volleyball pals that Ty loved. Her respite from the claustrophic Lee-controlled environment. Tinfoil even covered their trailer windows, Lee was so jealous.

Lee cooked the frozen dinners-for-one but ate earlier, alone. She watched warily while Ty and Sandy ate their turkey and enjoyed each other's company. Seven days later, Richard Mallory was dead.

With the money she stole, Lee reverted to her childhood strategy: trying to win friends by paying for beer and parties. Now it was beer, parties and rent.

The most glaring clue of all was Ty's sister Tracey's summer visit, slap bang in the middle of the killing year. The sisters' bond was like a knife in Lee's gut. She was petrified that Ty would move back to Ohio with Tracey. I know with every fibre of my being that fear tipped her. She couldn't allow *that*. In the three weeks Ty's sister stayed, Lee killed three men. A staggering escalation by any standards.

After one, she came home waving six one-hundred-dollar bills saying: Now we can have fun, I'll take us to SeaWorld, I'll pay the miserable old fucker who's on us for the rent.

Unaware of any murders, Tracey was nevertheless scared by Lee's gun and volatile personality. Anything could set the woman off. Smelling the trouble she was stirring, Tracey cut her vacation short.

Lee always craved fame and attention, wanted a book written about her. She had Bonnie and Clyde fantasies and a hatred for humanity that confounded her.

Finally, I felt sure of the "why?". Acts of serial murder often are preceded by stressors, some last personal straw. I believe that as a borderline personality, Lee's killing was triggered primarily by her ramped-up abandonment fears. I also strongly suspect that killing also spent some of her bottomless pit of anger.

Ultimately, Lee confessed to save Tyria, who wasn't involved in her crimes. To help police entrap Lee, Ty cried to her over the phone, saying she was afraid they were going to arrest her.

Lee's chilling confession tape showed little remorse.

It wasn't that my empathy for Lee was gone. Rather, despair descended. She seemed irredeemable. Thinking that will sink you.

Whatever others wanted for her and of her, Lee would kill again. She knew it. (She knew herself better than some thought.) I knew it. A jury knew it. Yet others refused to accept her truth.

"Of course she killed because that guy raped her!" "Bitch, it's obvious you've never been raped." Words spat my way by women. Much unquestioning support for Wuornos is surely born of the sympathy drummed up for the attack victim in *Monster*. But I learned how very loaded an issue psychopathy in women is for some females. Some, I suspect, are victims. Women who, having suffered themselves, project onto Aileen their own thoughts and ideas. A few even seem to believe that any man going to a prostitute deserves death.

Clearly, Lee became a repository for all kinds of projected ideas and unexpressed anger at men. For those unwilling to believe in the darkness of her psychic shadow, she is a heroic victim. So be it.

Interesting. Historically, men are just serial killers or murderous sonsofbitches. Yet women who kill are demonized with pejorative terms like black widows and angels of death. Hell hath no fury like a woman scorned, right?

Yet Lee wasn't a T-shirt slogan. To me, calling her a man-hating lesbian was an insult to gays. Tantamount to saying that only a hard-core dyke man-hater would kill this way, so we can ignore what Lee's crimes say about women's capacity for violence.

Irony is, Lee wasn't a lesbian according to the straight men with whom she willingly had sex and relationships. She was bisexual, more likely. She had two woman-to-woman relationships and sex with Tyria was a low priority. Too low, said Ty. And maybe the drain of hooking played into that. But the real power of Lee's pull to Ty was emotional—born of her ravenous need for love.

Another huge double standard is that paradoxically we are far more forgiving of women who kill than of men, while research shows that many such men likely endured childhood abuse too. There's near-unanimous revulsion at and condemnation of male serial killers. Who cares what they went through as kids? Lee, however, triggered empathy, forgiveness, understanding and protective maternal instincts. Her crimes were justified for her more energetically than she justified them herself. And her victims were demonized.

Finally, she blessed the victims' families with a longed-for, overdue admission: there was no rape, no self-defence. Richard Mallory definitely wasn't self-defence, she told documentarian Nick Broomfield, admitting that Mallory had the wheels she needed *and the amount of money*. Some folk seemed to feel betrayed (on camera, Broomfield seemed dumbfounded), closed to accepting the idea that the men she killed didn't hurt her.

For the biographer, to get past your empathy is the test. I confess it got easier. True equality demands that Aileen Wuornos be assessed as unflinchingly as any murderous male counterpart. And I found myself unwilling to sacrifice my belief in full equality to distort her into something she was not.

Writing true crime, you try to reconcile the humanity you have tapped into with the inescapable savagery of your subject's all too concrete actions. Only then can you bring your journey into another's mind to a somewhat peaceful resolution.

To me, Lee's victims were people. To her, they were a means to an end. Coffee tables.

Near execution day, decompensating emotionally after a decade of near-isolation, she spoke of the mothership transporting her. In a way it was very Lee, translating her ever-present bible in her own unique way. Complaining of abuse or her food being poisoned, yet keen to meet her maker. Some saw her as a mentally ill rape victim masticated by the system and her execution as the equivalent of the state killing a mentally retarded prisoner.

For me, it was more personally haunting. In Florida in 1992, just before she received her 2nd, 3rd and 4th death sentences, I stood in a sunlit, glassily modern courtroom corridor waiting for the inevitable yet surreal pronouncement. Not 'Good morning,' or 'Go to hell,' but word that Death Row was waiting, "until, by warrant of the Governor of the State of Florida, you, Aileen Carol Wuornos, be electrocuted until you are dead."

Thinking back on that day all these years later, I have to tell you, the words still kill me.

July 1969, thirteen-year-old Aileen Wuornos
smiling on an annual family holiday.

Photo from Sue Russell's Lethal Intent,
courtesy of Lori Grody

POEM FOR SOME WOMEN

huh?
  i'm all right
  i say i'm
  all right
what you lookin at?
  i say i'm all right
  doing ok
  i'm i'm i'm still
  writin producin on the radio
  who i fooling
  i'm just a little ill now
  just got a little jones
    jones jones jones
      habit habit habit

took my 7 yr old to
the crack house with me
on Thursday
beautiful girl.
prettiest little girl
her momma done ever seen
took her so she understand
why i late sometimes with
her breakfast dinner bedtime
meetings bedtime love.
Wanted her to know how
hard it is for me you
know a single woman
out here on her own you know
and so i took her to the
crack house where this
man. This dog this
former friend of mine lived

wudn't give me no crack
no action. Even when
i opened my thighs to give him some
him again for the umpteenth
time he said no all
the while looking at
my baby my pretty
little baby. And he
said i want her. i need
a virgin. Your stuff's
too loose you had
so much traffic up
there you could
park a truck up there
and still have room
for something else.
And he laughed. And he laughed.
And he laughed. This long laugh.
And i looked at him and the
stuff he wuz holding in his
hand and you know i cudn't
remember my baby's
name he held the stuff out
to me and i cudn't remember
her birthdate i cudn't remember
my daughter's face. And
i cried as i walked out that door.
   What's her name, puddintang
   ask me again and I'll tell
   you the same thing
cdn't even hear her
screaming my name as he
tore into her pretty little
panties

"prettiest little girl
you ever done seen
prettiest little mama's
baby you done ever seen."

Bought my baby this pretty
little leather jacket off the street
when i went to pick her up Sunday
7 days later i walked right
up to the house opened the
door and saw her sitting
on the floor she said Momma
where you been? Momma
Momma Momma Momma Momma.

Momma's little baby
loves shortening shortening
Momma's little baby
loves shortening bread
put on the jacket
put on the jacket
Momma's little baby
loves shortening bread

When we got home she
wudn't talk to me. She just
sat and stared. Wudn't watch
the t.v. when i turned it on.
When we got home she just
stared at me with her eyes
dog like. Just sat and
looked at me with her eyes til
i had to get outta there
you know.

My baby ran away
from home last week my sweet
little shortening bread ran
away from home last nite and
i dreamed she was dead
i dreamed she was
surrounded by panthers who
tossed her back and forth nibbling
and biting and tearing her up. My little shortening bread ran
away from home last week.
peekaboo i see you and
you and you and you
and you. do you see me?

FOR ALICE NOTLEY

Seeing you take the stage
slump-backed
        belly forward
                in
a no-nonsense
        green or beige dress
the very image
        of the lady poet
of the ages
        a latter day Leonie
    or Louise
    or Marianne

I recall a winter day in '68
running into you
        at the Gotham Book Mart
as you climbed
        from that cavern
I was about to climb
            down into—
a lithe young woman in black
        black-stockinged
        A look you had down pat
          too

I wouldn't have bet on you
        for the Los Angeles Times
           Poetry Award
but thought you were beautiful
        and mysterious
though a bit aloof
        and wondered at you gone off
with my older friend
        Ted

That was thirty years ago
before this night when I meet
your beautiful sister
                    and her family
and your husband Doug Oliver
your sons with Ted
            Anselm and Edmund
                                grown up
            and you emerged
            A late eminence

How proud Ted would be!
How much he was eased
            by you, Alice
            in the dark passage
            of the fifteen years
                        you gave him
before he died
                    in New York
            on a scorching 4th of July

It was after that
            that you pulled up
            from your depths
the story of a family
            no one
                        could have guessed
from Needles, California
            the national black madness
going back to Vietnam
            and a brother's fate

It's the blink of an eye
            to traverse the thirty years
though they came
                        slowly
            with their cargoes of
                        pleasure and pain

Some people turn themselves
       inside out
surely a poet's chore
       to render the story
time tells
       on the body
       we all are

And you are such a one
eyes so much fuller than
when you used the black kohl
little slits of mirth and grief
I greet you again, old friend
in the turn of the years
and thank you
           for the good faith
       of your climb
       from the cavern
       to the stage

Aram Saroyan

CEO DISEASE

In his history of the means and methods of mass communication, Marshall McLuhan underscored the power of machines and electronic media to influence human perception. Among his many startling ideas was his assertion that Hitler could not have had the impact that he had without the invention of the radio and his mastery in that medium. He said virtually the same of Franklin Delano Roosevelt, with his tradition of presidential "fireside chats" broadcast over the radio. While Hitler created the Third Reich and the Nazi Holocaust, Roosevelt grappled with the Depression and brought America through it, in the process taking the nation to war to help defeat Hitler. One sees here that a single invention, utilized masterfully by two world leaders, can yield cosmically different results: on the one hand unprecedented suffering and human carnage, and on the other a revived economy and increased social justice.

With the apotheosis of the industrial epoch experienced in the twentieth century came a simultaneous exfoliation of new diseases related to the effects of industry on the environment and its human, animal and vegetal populations. The green-house effect, global warming, the extinction of various wildlife species, and the many forms of cancer related to industrial waste in the air, water, soil, and by extension animal and vegetable food products, are signatures—some might say *the* signature—of this epoch. We are changing the conditions upon which life on our planet is based, and yet there is a predictable outcry from corporate leaders whenever an effort is made to contain the damage.

Anyone might reasonably ask what's going on. Yet oddly the question is seldom heard. If, for example, a neighbor were to set fires that caused damage to his and his neighbors' homes, steps would be taken in short order—from calling the police and fire department to enlisting social services to address the neighbor's behavior. Instead, we have a curiously sheepish attitude toward the corporate CEO. It was reported that Michael Eisner, the CEO of Disney, received in 1998 a salary equal to $278,500 an hour. It's certain that Bill Gates of Microsoft makes even more money. A sum of money of this magnitude is more than anyone needs—and this at the same time that millions of children in our nation go hungry each day.

Several years ago Bill Gates responded to a public outcry about his wealth by donating large sums from his fortune to charity. It's probable that Mr. Eisner has his own charities. But the inequity of the wealth of these leaders set beside the poverty of other citizens and their children is a question that deserves deeper scrutiny than it has yet received.

There are now 350 billionaires on the planet who have as much wealth as half the world's population. These are individuals who have as much wealth as nations. The question is why. What could these 350 people need with such wealth? The Nader 2000 campaign brought up for the first time in my memory the idea of a maximum wage, as a natural counterpart to the minimum wage. The idea was barely reported along with the rest of his campaign. Was the campaign so poorly covered *because* of such ideas? Is an idea like a maximum wage communism? Surely it would be attacked as such by any candidate opposed to it.

But isn't it time we got beyond these hobgoblins and addressed the reality of a geo-political crisis? The nature of the crisis, the undeclared war if you will, is no longer national in character but global. It pits the citizen against the multi-national corporation, and guess which side has the upper hand?

One wonders if there now exists a recognizable species of pathology, a psychological counterpart of the proliferation of physical diseases that has marked our era, that might conveniently be labeled CEO Disease.

Years ago Tom Cruise made a small but heartening gesture. While making the film "Born on the Fourth of July," based on the autobiography of Ron Kovic, who had returned from the Vietnam

War paralyzed from the waist down, he appointed Mr. Kovic his advisor on the role and paid him one percent of his salary. Among bona fide Chief Executive Officers, George Soros and Ted Turner are two who have voluntarily made generous gifts on behalf of the public welfare.

On the other hand, a corporate CEO had a heart attack some years ago. After recovering he encountered an acquaintance who reported that he also had had a heart attack.

"Well, yes," the CEO said. "But my heart attack was much more serious than yours."

In Twelve Step Recovery programs, it's said that a person doesn't begin to recover until he or she hits bottom. The problem with CEO Disease is that the CEO may not reach bottom before the wholesale destruction of our eco-system.

What can be done about it? To return to Mr. McLuhan: He said there was no inevitability so long as there was a willingness to consider alternatives. One step in that direction, it strikes me, would be to make the issue a part of public discourse.

BAGHDAD APOLLINAIRE

My mouth is a fully automatic weapon
the telephone is an outgrowth of my mind
Let your friends in on it, they're about to reinstate
the draft in between commercials for SUVs
O prophetic television, something is rotten in Denmark
bombs, metal flowers blooming, nascent
consciousness. Humankind, kings are awakening
to no clothes, where are your pants Lothario?
Citizen Bush, I feel the need to question even familiar things
in light of the afternoon's vice grip on sanity.
Government principles now have more to do with simple extortion
nasturtium, napalm, General Custer, moon or skull above the waste
allotments?
I saw the best minds of my generation yawning
where the dawn's specious reliquary breaks resplendent.
I'm packing my bags to make the move to Venus.
My mouth is a fully automatic weapon
rising upward as the horizon shifts to nausea.
This, crepuscular world, is my canticle to peace.
You won't wrench this flower from *my* grasp, etc.
meantime wake-up, change the channel—

notice earthbound meteor.

Eabhan Ní Shuileabháin

IMITATIO DEI IN SAN QUENTIN

1. Watch Lieutenant

I check with the watch officers
all through the night,
watch the tenseness develop
in the way Jimmy cracks his knuckles,
the way Don's right eye twitches.
At eight minutes to ten
I unlock his cell,
ask him to take off his clothes.
He always knows exactly what to do.
I give him blue jeans and a white shirt.

We all keep a careful distance apart,
so conscious of nearness
that our limbs become mechanized,
straight and only one-jointed,
our arms stuck to our sides and
our legs taking slow deliberate steps.
We tend to stare just past one another,
keep our sentences short and soft-spoken.
My whole body aches for days afterward.

2. Chamber Operator

Somebody has to do it.
If it's not me, it'll be somebody else,
and at least I'm just doing a job—
not like some in this business.

It's the warden who orders me—
At two and a half minutes past ten,
I remove the safety pin and
depress the mechanical action.
Cyanide gas is released inside the chamber.

It's much more humane than the chair, you know?
I wouldn't operate the chair.
Don't much like the lethal injection either.
Too finicky, too many needles.
Too many ways to make a mistake—
Imagine missing the vein.
As for the firing squad—yeah, yeah, it still exists,
they did it a couple of years back, in Utah, I think—
people just don't like it. Barbaric, I suppose,
too much blood and guts leaking out.
No, gas is the best way.

3. OFFICIAL WITNESS

I covered Somalia a few years ago,
so thought this would be easy.
But fuck, the violence is worse here.
Over there, it was random,
just a bunch of thugs with guns.
Here, everyone knows how it's going to happen,
where it's going to happen,
when it's going to happen—
and everyone just waits for the show.

To get through it,
I focus on how everyone else reacts.
I check the clock,
I look at the guards' faces,

watch who's coming through the door,
stopwatch how long it all takes.

One thing for sure.
It's all made to look as unlike murder as possible.

4. WARDEN

I know these men's cases inside out,
Am aware of every exhausted appeal.

When it is time,
I order the execution to proceed.
I am only the mouthpiece of the state,
making sure the will of the people is done.

5. MEDICAL OFFICER

I only do this because it's part of my job
And usually my job allows me to help these guys.

It only takes 30 seconds before he's unconscious.
Ten minutes later, I confirm he's dead.

I complete his death certificate.

6. CONTROL SERGEANT

I have nothing glamorous to do.
All I do is subtract one from the institutional count.
Can't have a corpse as part of the general population, now can we?

DREAMS MAY COME

Growing up in a small town is great, I guess, if you're like everyone else. But I'm not, and it's messing me up. I never have a moment's peace.

Actually that's not quite true. Some summer nights up under the roof, looking out the little window of the attic, it's almost like flying. My mind flutters from porchlight to porchlight over the town and out over the cornfields and soybeans. There's usually a light over the irrigation pumps. The world of plants is cold and alien, but it's less scary than people, and I don't mind it if there's a light on.

I first noticed it in church, during sermons and during offertory. All those *thoughts,* caught between Luther's urging to take joy in the gifts of the flesh and the unspoken but stronger teaching that all joys are dangers. All those eyes locked on breasts and butts while we stand there singing hymns. Makes me feel dirty. Makes me feel stuck to the ground. I can't let go and fly over the music the way I used to. I feel like I'm participating in something bad, against my will.

In school, I'm a good enough student. The athletes sit next to me because I don't care if they cheat off me. Sophomore year, and it's the same story, until now, second semester. Something's in the air. In biology, I get that feeling again. Like I'm grounded. I have to struggle to understand the lectures. The guy next to me won't sit still. He squirms in his seat the whole class period.

It started the second semester of my sophomore year. I remember because I had just made starting team in basketball. Everything worked out. I got seated next to someone smart in English, geometry, and biology. Coach taught world history. So no problem with grades. But these dreams about wrecked it. And I'm not the kind of guy who pays attention to stuff like dreams. I don't think I even ever had dreams before that season.

Every week, it seems to get worse. Sometimes my mind is cloudy for hours after biology. It's getting so it won't ever clear up. It just builds up like a big thunderhead. A big cloud with flashes of images. A girl's breast. A finger sliding into a vagina. Not the kinds of things I normally think about. A hand around a cock, pulling on it, pulling it out of the body. My eyes zoom in on the skin. Golden-brown pubic hairs. Purple velvet cockhead. Weeping cockslit. Bloody hands.

It wouldn't quit all night. I'd dream I was running laps or driving tractor or throwing freethrows. But always having to look behind, like someone was back there, breathing on my neck. It seemed like I'd be doing this for days, but then I would wake up and the clock radio would say 2:30 a.m. I'd lay there staring into the dark and it felt like something was pressing into my brain. Not painful, just pushing. So I'd fall asleep in class and get detention and be late for practice.

I didn't say before, that when I was laying there in bed awake, all I could think about was my dick. I'd touch it, squeeze it, stroke it. I'd jerk off all night till it was all raw in places. I would be practically crying. I felt like I was going to tear my dick right off. But I couldn't come.

The only way I can concentrate now is to allow that cock into my mind. I focus on it, crawl across it like a fly. I'm gaining more control and creeping up the torso—through those almost invisible hairs. I reach the face and zoom out. It's him!

Now at least I have a reason to go to school. I start studying him mentally as we sit. I don't know what the link was between us. Sometimes he looks like the sky when it's green, right before the tails of tornados start descending. This is why my mind flies away from people. Sometimes I feel like I could turn into this "Creature Feature" thing and walk through town throwing cars at houses and picking people up and sticking them in my mouth.

Finally mid-season, nighttime was torture. Mom and Dad wanted to take me to the doctor. Coach just said I was jerking off too much. I wasn't sure if he was kidding or not, but he moved me to second string. The same dreams. One night I was sitting on a bench in a big empty room when I felt whatever it was in back of me. I didn't look back, I just grabbed. Someone's arms were around me and picking me up, holding me like a baby. I looked up, but my eyes were all blurry and the face seemed so far away. He seemed familiar though. He was stroking the bottom of my thighs and kind of making baby sounds at me. Then he started feeling my butt. I was squirming around, but he was really holding on to me. He stroked my thighs. It was a strange feeling, hot and wet and rough, like a tongue. Then between my thighs, then toward my butt. I could feel my dick crawling up my belly. He started in, till he reached my hole. Then stopped. He pressed up and down on my hole, without going in. I was holding my dick in both hands and nursing from it. My butt would tighten up then relax. He pressed in, then electricity ran from his finger or tongue through my guts, through my mouth, into my dick. It was like lightning.

Then suddenly, one day the sky clears. I can fly again. He's released something and is sleeping again. I'm sitting next to him and I can see a golden light pulsing from his seat right up through his body—from his ass—to his face. He almost has a halo.

Marc Smith

DETENTION CENTER

Somewhere, while we speak, while we sip our coffee Boston in the cabarets and cafes discussing the issues of freedom and restraint, Art and Liberty . . . somewhere, in the third world, a father, separated from family and friends, stands facing a concrete wall. He hears his son cry out,

"Poppy!"

and hammers a dark spot with a red fist; his soul trying to rip itself free from body to fly around the wall, to go through it, to break it down.

"Poppy!"

The man is any man. The circumstances of such a life as his we've been lucky to avoid. We cannot know him. We cannot understand him. We can only imagine how his soul erupts in his throat, tears at his mind, and flexes the flesh and fiber of his useless muscle. We can only imagine his forehead pressed against the aggregate, knocking against the concrete wall, in a room of concrete walls, in a room of fathers aggregated together, pressed into circumstances, hearing their children cry out:

"Poppy!"

Our discussions are important. Our concern is real. But as we sip the black anger of our comfortable homes, milking the repression of our easy existence, stirring the sweet and sour soundings of our still free voice into teacup whirlpools of angst and depression, somewhere, in the third world, a man stands facing a concrete wall pounding his fist raw into the hopelessness unable to do what he must do, unable to be, unable to free his soul to fly around the wall, to go through it, to break it down.

"Poppy"

The cry is not of a nation. The cry is not of one breed above another, or one thought over the rest, or one god more god than all the gods it would suppress. It is the cry of any son who needs his father, of any woman who must suckle her young, of any life that needs to live free. And as we sip our coffee and swill our beers watching our leisure hours dissipate into dull days of disappointment having become too self-absorbed and sophisticated to believe in the nobility of dreams once dreamed when lips cried out with ideal passion,

"Poppy!"

As we espresso our abstractions against imagined barriers, somewhere, in the third world, a man, a woman, separated from family and friends, stand facing a concrete wall hearing the children they cannot save cry:

"Poppy!"

Carolyn Stoloff

SLIDES

I give you an untamed afternoon blowing blackbirds off course
    Clerks chase a yellow memo through the park

I give you a checkered afternoon
    In Chicago where men play shoving games a tall man
        pours a waterfall of cards from one hand to the other

I give you an afternoon clogged with names—those tacks
    boys hold at the apex of slings
        Could you predict the leap of a grasshopper?

It's afternoon—the professor races past shops looking for
    a clock—he's late
        Students tethered to a table like small craft, wait
        to be loaded

I give you an office afternoon—at his desk *Time*'s editor
    navigates vacated events, a river with eddies of
    conflicting rumor
        On it an olive leaf floats

I give you a Mediterranean afternoon with blue houses
    Oh Leonardo, I would walk beside you through eternity
        debating at what angle one wall becomes another!

At noon a widow spreads her wet handkerchief on a wall
    And a heaviness in me rose like a helmet of water
        from a deep well

Street sweepers sweep noon's chaff into narrow shadow-creeks
    A girl with white arms fits rusty hooks into shutters
        making dusk

I give you a good afternoon
    An old woman carries a spoonful of soup to an old man
        who nods in the shade of an olive tree

FOR SYLVIA*

For Sylvia, a million kisses.
Few are hits: most are misses.
What chance has a superstar
To hear the far-off praises?
She glides in starlight radiance,
A nebula of gravity
Dazzling! points of light condensed
To diamond clarity.
She sparkles in the universe
Aglow with life and wit and mirth
Her levity's alarming! In short
She's simply charming. She conquers
Where the strong are wont
Merely to survive.

*See Sylvia Miles' poem for Nelson Sullivan on page 139

Mark Terrill

THE VAGARIES

Tangier, Boulevard Pasteur,
walking back to the Hotel Lutetia
on a wet October evening.

Nervous gusts slicing in off the strait,
rain drumming against closed shutters . . .

Paul Bowles dead and buried in upstate New York,
William Burroughs dead and buried in Kansas,
Alfred Chester gone crazy and gone . . .

Mohammed Mrabet ensconced on his farm,
Madame Porte's Tea Room
closed down and boarded up . . .

This ghostliness
is very real.
As real as
shadows and light
and the loaded interstices
in between.

The title of tonight's experiment is
"The Vagaries of Transience."

My thesis will be delivered tomorrow at noon
at the Caves of Hercules

where a white scorpion
waits trembling
under a shiny black rock.

DECEMBER, OUTDOORS

Clouds like fish shedding scales are stretched thin

above Salem. The calm cold sea

accepts the sun as an equal, a match:

the horizon a truce, the air all still.

Sun, but no shadows somehow, the trees

ideally deleafed, a contemplative gray

that ushers into the woods (in summer

crammed with undergrowth) sheer space.

How fortunate it is to move about

without impediment, Nature having

no case to make, no special weather to plead,

unlike some storm-obsessed old symphonist.

The day is *piano*; I see buds so subtle

they know, though fat, that this is no time to bloom.

Gerard Van der Leun

VICTIMS OF THE PLAGUE

for Thom Gunn

Perhaps our dances, in a thousand years,
will tattooed be as drums,
And our bright minds, forged by fate,
will in the musk of eons drown.

Our souls will all rise glorified
as a pod of whales weaves waves.
Our flesh, once firm, relaxed as stones
that serve to mark our graves.

Our pleasures seen as ancient rites
describable as dreams;
Our voices, in a million years,
insubstantial as starbeams.

Perhaps our minuets, in a billion years,
will as steel stiffened be.
Our arabesques as smooth and gestural
as drowned paintings of the sea.

Our nods but inclinations
of the folds beneath the eyes.
Our plans but vague intentions
of the wind beneath the skies.

Our breath, a transpiration
of dust immured in dust.
Our lives, a visitation
of a rush light drowned in musk.

All these, our words and scattered songs,
May come, in time, to less than naught,
As Mayan blocks of hard hacked stone
Embalm the skin we once sloughed off.

But now, like rattles kept within
A jeweled bone box, our hollowed skin
Is shaken in the rambles of the park
To frighten schoolgirls after dark.

François Villon

BALLADE

Hommes faillis despourveuz de raison
Desnaturez et hors de congnoissance
Desmis du sens, comblez de desraison
Fols abusez plains de descongnoissance
Qui procurez contre vostre naissance
Vous soubzmettans a detestable mort
Par lascheté, las, que ne vous remort
L'orribleté qui a honte vous maine
Voyez comment maint jeunes homs est mort
Par offenser et prendre autruy demaine.

Chascun en soy voye sa mesprison
Ne nous venjons, prenons en pacience
Nous congnoissons que ce monde est prison
Aux vertueux franchis d'impatience
Battre, rouiller, pour ce n'est pas science
Tollir, ravir, piller, meurtrir a tort
De Dieu ne chault, trop de verté se tort
Qui en telz faiz sa jeunesse demaine
Dont a la fin ses poins doloreux tort
Par offenser et prendre autruy demaine.

Que vault piper, flater, rire en trayson
Quester, mentir, affermer sans fiance
Farcer, tromper, artifier poison
Vivre en pechié, dormir en deffiance
De son prouchain sans avoir confiance?
Pour ce conclus, de bien faisons effort
Reprenons cuer, ayons en Dieu confort
Nous n'avons jour certain en la sepmaine
De nos maulx ont noz parens le ressort
Par offenser et prendre autruy demaine.

François Villon
—Translated by **Galway Kinnell**

BALLADE

You lost men deaf to reason
Unnatural, fallen from knowledge
Emptied of sense, filled with unreason
Deluded fools stuffed with ignorance
Who hire out against your birthright
You give yourselves to detestable death
Through cowardice, alas, why no remorse
For the monstrousness dragging you into shame?
Think of all the young men who've met death
By injuring and taking from others.

Let each find the guilt in his own heart
Let us not take revenge but be patient
We know this world is a prison
For righteous men freed from impatience
Therefore it's stupid to fight and brawl
Steal, rape, pillage, kill wrongfully
Whoever spends his youth at these things
Cares not for God, abandons virtue
And at last wrings his hands in sorrow
By injuring and taking from others.

What good to plot, flatter, laugh falsely
Sell indulgences, lie, pledge in bad faith
Hustle, cheat, concoct poison
Live in sin, sleep in suspicion
Of your neighbor and trust no one?
So I say we should strive for the good
Take heart and find strength in God
For us not a day of the week is secure
Our families get the brunt of our blows
By injuring and taking from others.

Vivons en paix, exterminons discort
Ieunes et vieulx, soyons tous d'ung accort
La loy le veult, l'apostre le ramaine
Licitement en l'epistre rommaine
Ordre nous fault, estat ou aucun port
Notons ces poins, ne laissons le vray port
Par offenser et prendre autruy demaine.

Vanquish discord, live in peace
Ioin* in agreement young and old
Law commands it, the Apostle in his
Letter to the Romans explicitly urges it
Order is necessary, rank, something to fall back on
Note all this, don't leave the safe harbor
By injuring and taking from others.

*As classical Latin has no letter "J" and uses "I" for both "I" and "J"
sounds, Kinnell does as Villon did, when pressed to find an "I" to fulfill
the acrostic. Thus the word formed is "Join" though it looks like "Ioin",
just as Villon's word is "Jeunes" though it looks like "Ieunes".

Two Doves. Photography by Itzhak Ben-Arieh (www.ben-arieh.com)
Photomontage, Israel, 1993
Courtesy Itzhak Ben-Arieh Collection

TOPOGRAPHY

"He was one more incognito in the city of illustrious incognitos."
—*Bon Voyage, Mr. President,* Gabriel García Márquez

The same substance, your bones.
Think protection, rockets—safe, gala crowd faces.

The republic has arrived. The market
is booming with traitors. Time to blend
your pistons with Manjusri[1],
the sword still evenly bends you.

Outside, the wreck is still curling into itself.
Lizards slide between bank doors.
Energy from Wichita, scaffolds of eyes.
You put me here in Oz. I'm not the first
serpent with sapphire slippers to kiss
the compass. I'm recording this into my skin—
every time the flytrap cuts up the language.
Every time you redress me. You make me
inflatable. Cavernous and plain.

Next time, streets in August, a pallid, familiar
name, notice your extinction. Notice mine.

Recognize this blue non-

Lastly,

"No dramas, no mantras, no striving will I let by me.
Those who are ready shall pass.
The rest shall strive, dissatisfied and fight among themselves,
letting their true natures come to the surface and wonder,
'why was I not chosen?'"[2]

---

[1] Bodhisattva with Discriminating Sword of Wisdom
[2] Excerpt from *Songs and Meditations of the Tibetan Dhyani Buddhas*

Phillip Ward

HUNGER HUNGER IT RAGES
for Phyllis Lee, 1952–2003

hunger hunger it rages
it rages on extreme
every direction a madness
with life tethered on a fragile string
and a handful of sleeping pills
a glass of water to swallow them
and one final glance around the room
her childhood-crowded room
drinking in the views of each wall
a collage of self-preservation and conceptual desire
a vivid expression of a saddened heart
a crowded tapestry of love to all then
her perception blared outward blurry-eyed
sweeping in rapid motion desire
one last swallow of water
one last roundabout view
one last drink of life
then she went off to sleep one last time
her body becoming wintry cold
she slept away a quiet rage and willingly
let death take hold massaging her heart to eternal rest
she slept the long night through to be found
alone and undressed for fate
arms open and welcoming death
hunger hunger raged on inside her
the fragile string snapped clear

leading her toward

a cloud of pale gray dust

on an eastern kentucky mountainside

where ash glittering in the sky

carpets land where daisies will bloom

hunger hunger it rages

every direction a madness

it rages on extreme

hunger hunger

missing

her

Phyllis Lee, Paintsville Lake, 1991. Photo by Phillip Ward (www.crisperanto.org).
"Phyllis Lee was my favorite of thirteen siblings," says Ward. "In 1991, at Paintsville
Lake, Kentucky, I said to her that she looked like Alice Cooper in drag. 'Be real, honey!'
she said, then struck this captured pose. Phyllis Lee was real to the end."

Copyright © 2005 by Phillip Ward

Karen Weiser

STILL LIFE WITH TYPEWRITER
AND SPEEDED-UP SNOW

Slow sex expose
     the personal economy

          balance on your hind legs
bubble terrain

to grasp the moneybag
     dupe

          calm closed and flat
gray heap of human levels

one light
     its eye-duplicate

          blurry with graspability
ashen round win

FISH

On the sidewalk in front
of a hair-dresser's supply store
lay the head of a fish,
largish, pointy, perhaps a pike's.

It must recently have been left there;
its scales shone and its visible eye
had enough light left in it still
so it looked as they will for awhile

astonished and disconsolate
to have been brought to such a pass:
its incision was clean, brutal, precise;
it had to have come in one blow.

In the show-case window behind,
other heads, women's and men's,
bewigged, painstakingly coiffed,
stared out, as though at the fish,

as though stunned, aghast, too—
though they were hardly surprised:
hadn't they known all along
that life, that frenzy, that folly,

that flesh-thing, would come
sooner or later to this? It hurts,
life, just as much as it might,
and it ends, always, like this.

Better stay here, with eyes of glass,
like people in advertisements,
and without bodies or blood,
like people in poems.

Daisy Zamora

CUANDO LAS VEO PASAR

Cuando las veo pasar alguna vez me digo: qué sentirán
ellas, las que decidieron ser perfectas conservar a toda costa
sus matrimonios no importa cómo les haya resultado el marido
(parrandero mujeriego jugador pendenciero
gritón violento penqueador lunático raro algo anormal
neurótico temático de plano insoportable
dundeco mortalmente aburrido bruto insensible desaseado
ególatra ambicioso desleal politiquero ladrón traidor mentiroso
violador de las hijas verdugo de los hijos emperador de la casa
tirano en todas partes) pero ellas se aguantaron
y sólo Dios que está allá arriba sabe lo que sufrieron.

Cuando las veo pasar tan dignas y envejecidas
los hijos las hijas ya se han ido en la casa sólo ellas han quedado
con ese hombre que alguna vez quisieron (tal vez ya se calmó
no bebe apenas habla se mantiene sentado frente al televisor
anda en chancletas bosteza se duerme ronca se levanta temprano
está achacoso cegato inofensivo casi niño) me pregunto:

¿Se atreverán a imaginarse viudas a soñar alguna noche que son
    libres
y que vuelven por fin sin culpas a la vida?

Daisy Zamora
—Translated by **George Evans**

WHEN I SEE THEM PASSING BY

When I see them passing by I ask myself sometimes: What must
they feel, the ones who decided to be perfect and keep their marriages
afloat against all odds no matter how their husbands turned out
(party animal womanizer gambler troublemaker
loud-mouthed violent headbanger lunatic weirdo slightly abnormal
neurotic obsessive clearly unbearable
dumbbell deadly boring brute insensitive grubby
egomaniacal ambitious disloyal politicker crook traitor liar
rapist of daughters torturer of sons emperor of the house
tyrant everywhere) but they put up with it
and God only knows what they suffered.

When I see them passing by so dignified and aged
their sons and daughters gone from the house leaving them alone
with a man they once loved (perhaps he's calmed down
doesn't drink hardly talks spends his time with TV
walks in slippers yawns falls asleep snores wakes up early
is ailing harmless almost childish) I ask myself:

Do they dare imagine themselves widows dreaming some night they are
    free
and coming at last without guilt back to life?

Harriet Zinnes

LIGHT LIGHT or THE CURVATURE OF THE EARTH

The light that shines from your eyes
shudders my vision;
opens a world that is an opulent sea,
a forest of trees,
a sky with flocks of roving birds,
a river where fish dwell,
where sea urchins with their protruding spines
echo the radiating waters.
Light light,
eyes eyes,
vision that is sun
that empowers the rollicking earth.

Light, light,
empower me!
I am roaming. I am looking.
Empower me—now!
Light, light.
Now!

NOTHING IS SECRET

It is foreknowledge, after all.
Nothing is secret.
Transparency rules.
Fortunes rise and fall,
and the buttermilk sours
even as the lamps go out
and the swimmer arrives at the shore.

If you have a story,
tell it.
Let it be a romance
with a happy ending.
Even the raped hold hands,
even a child romps in the fields.

Beware, beware,
the snake is sliding on the grass;
the plane has lost its wing.

GALWAY COUNTY LIBRARIES

CONTRIBUTORS' NOTES ✍

MAYA ANGELOU (www.mayaangelou.com) was born Marguerite Johnson in St. Louis, Missouri, on April 4, 1928. She grew up in St. Louis and Stamps, Arkansas. Dr. Angelou is an author, poet, historian, songwriter, playwright, dancer, stage and screen producer, director, performer, singer, and civil rights activist. In addition to her bestselling autobiographies, beginning with *I Know Why the Caged Bird Sings* (1969), which was nominated for the National Book Award, she has also written numerous volumes of poetry, including *Just Give Me a Cool Drink of Water 'fore I Diiie* (1971), which was nominated for the Pulitzer Prize, and *Wouldn't Take Nothing for My Journey Now* (1993), as well as the celebrated poem "On the Pulse of Morning," which she read at the inauguration of President William Jefferson Clinton, and "A Brave and Startling Truth," written at the request of the United Nations and read at its fiftieth anniversary. In 1981, Dr. Angelou accepted a lifetime appointment as Reynolds Professor of American Studies at Wake Forest University in Winston-Salem, North Carolina, where she currently resides. ✍ **MOHAMMAD SHAMSUL AREFIN**, born 14 August 1980 in Dhaka, Bangladesh, took basic courses at Shuborno-Bijoy Art School in Dhaka, then moved to Malaysia to study Film Animation. He began working in Digital Art full time after moving to Malaysia. "I love doing photo manipulation," Arefin says. "It's one of my specialties." His artwork can be found on http://attar-khoje.deviantart.com and www.anirban.com. ✍ **COLIN ASKEY** (www.colinaskey.com) is a Louis Vuitton model and self-taught artist whose paintings have been exhibited in Paris, France, and in Calgary, Canada, where he's originally from. He has directed, written, and produced a heartwarming short film which will soon be available at thestrykerz.com. ✍ **MARGARET ATWOOD** (www.owtoad.com) was born in Ottawa on November 18, 1939, and grew up in northern Quebec and Ontario, and later in Toronto. She received her undergraduate degree from Victoria College at the University of Toronto and her master's degree from Radcliffe College. She is the recipient of numerous honours, such as The Sunday Times Award for Literary Excellence in the U.K., the National Arts Club Medal of Honor for Literature in the U.S., Le Chevalier dans l'Ordre des Arts et des Lettres in France, and she was the first winner of the London Literary Prize. She has received honorary degrees from universities across Canada, and one from Oxford University in England. An international literary star and one of Canada's most celebrated writers, Ms. Atwood is the author of more than thirty-five books of fiction, short stories, poetry, literary criticism, social history and books for children. Some of her best-known novels include *The Edible Woman* (1970), *The Handmaid's Tale* (1983), *The Robber Bride* (1994), *Alias Grace* (1996) and the 2000 Booker Prize winner, *The Blind Assassin*. Her latest novel is the stunning and provocative *Oryx and Crake*. She lives in Toronto with novelist Graeme Gibson. They have, "altogether," three grown children and a cat. ✍ **MICHELLE AUERBACH**'s prose, poetry, and translations have recently appeared in *Chelsea*, *American Drivel Review*, *Bombay Gin*, and the anthology *Sacred Stones* (Adams Media). Her book, *Alice Modern*

(Excessive Poetics Press), is due out this spring. ✍ **ELIZABETH AYRES** is the author of *Writing the Wave* and *The Ultimate Creative Writing Workshop*, as well as the founder of *The Elizabeth Ayres Center for Creative Writing* (www.Creative WritingCenter.com). She lives on a cattle ranch in northern New Mexico with 2 cats, 96 cows, and a variable number of calves each spring. ✍ **IAN AYRES**, founder and editor of *Van Gogh's Ear* (www.frenchcx.com), began writing poetry at puberty in houses of ill fame. In 1982, Leona Helmsley fired him from his desk clerk job at Helmsley Palace (New York City) for writing a poem on the back of Elizabeth Taylor's autograph in the hotel's celebrity guestbook. Since then, his poems and short stories have appeared internationally in hundreds of publications. Ayres moved from the U.S.A. to France in 1989 and, ten years later, along with Eric Elléna, created the movie production company French Connection Films, for which he wrote the screenplay *Killing Your Parents*, currently in production. Ayres' new book of poems, *Private Parts* (French Connection Press), will be released in May, 2005. ✍ **JOE BACAL** was Creative Director of Sunbow Entertainment for twenty years and in the early eighties, he was Head Writer of the Peabody Award winning TV series, *The Great Space Coaster.* He has lectured on creativity at the *Parsons School of Design* and is co-author of the satirical book, *How To Become A Legend In Your Own Lifetime—A New Concept in Self-Help*. His poems have recently appeared or are forthcoming in *Hanging Loose, JEWS Magazine, Mudfish*, and *Poetry New Zealand.* ✍ **AMANDA BAY** is a psychotherapist from California who now lives in Paris. Her work has appeared in *Pharos*. She is the mother of two young children. ✍ **ITZHAK BEN-ARIEH** (www.ben-arieh.com) was born in 1926 in Geneva of parents from Turkish origin. While in Geneva, he completed studies in Mechanical Engineering. Since moving to Israel in 1948, Ben-Arieh had been a member of a kibbutz, a metal worker, a practical engineer, and also a teacher of technological subjects in professional high schools. Only later, at the age of 45, did he discover the magic of photography, change profession and join the photographic laboratory of the Faculty of Architecture (Technion–Haifa) where he worked for 28 years. Ben-Arieh mainly employs the method of photomontage. His photographs have been part of major exhibitions all over the world. The National Library in Paris has acquired twelve of the artist's photographs. ✍ **DAVID BERGMAN**, a professor of English at Towson University in Baltimore, has become a significant figure in gay literature. Professor Bergman is the editor of *Camp Grounds, The Violet Quill Reader*, and the *Men on Men* series. In 1991 he published a seminal work of gay literary criticism, *Gaiety Transfigured: Gay Self-Representation in American Literature*. His books of poetry include *Heroic Measures* and *Cracking the Code*, which won the 1985 George Elliston Poetry Prize, from the Elliston Foundation at the University of Cincinnati. His most recent book is *The Violet Hour: The Violet Quill and the Making of Gay Culture* (Columbia University Press, 2004). ✍ **BILL BERKSON** is a poet, critic and professor of Liberal Arts at the San Francisco Art Institute. His most recent books of poetry are *Fugue State* and *Serenade* (both available from Small Press Distribution, Berkeley, CA). A collection of his criticism, *The Sweet Singer of Modernism & Other Art Writings 1985-2003*, was published in 2004 by Qua Books. ✍ **J. J. BLICKSTEIN** is a native New Yorker, poet/visual artist, and the editor/publisher of *Hunger Magazine* (www.hungermagazine.com). He lives in Upstate New York next to the Esopus River with a lovely biologist/herbalist and three kids. He works as a stone mason/handyman and occasionally teaches about the tarot. His chapbook, *Visions of Salt & Water,* is available from Bagatela Press (2003) and his book, *Barefoot on a drawing of the Sun,* is available from Fish Drum Inc. (2004). His work has appeared in numerous international journals, as well as in major anthologies such as: *The Subterraneans* (Poet's Gallery Press, 1998), *American Diaspora: Poetry of Displacement* (U. of Iowa Press, 2001), and *Shamanic Warriors, Now Poets* (R&R Publishing, Scotland, 2004). ✍ **PAT BRIEN** is British and has had countless articles published in various independent magazines in England, as well as several literary short-stories and a dramatic monologue broadcast on BBC radio. One of his literary stories has just been published in the United States, in the annual literary journal *The Long Story*, and one of his screenplays recently reached the semi-finals of Francis Ford Coppola's American Zoetrope Screenplay Contest. He currently writes articles for American francophile internet magazine *Bonjour Paris* (www.bonjourparis.com). He lives and works in Paris, France. ✍ **MARY BURGER** is a writer and editor living in Oakland, California. Recent writing appears in *Aufgabe*. She is co-editor of *Biting the Error: Writers on Experimental Narrative*, an anthology of work from the *Narrativity* website, forthcoming from Coach House Press in 2004. Also forthcoming is her novella *Sonny*, a story of a boy who accidentally witnesses the first atom bomb test. ✍ **CAROLYN CASSADY**, born Carolyn Robinson in April 1923, Nashville, Tennessee, is an acclaimed painter, set designer for the theatre, and writer. In 1947, at Colorado's University of Denver—where she was getting her MA degree in Theater and Fine Arts—Carolyn's life changed forever as she met future counterculture hero Neal Cassady. On April Fool's Day 1948, they were married, and eventually had three children. Early stages of Neal Cassady's involvement with Carolyn were fictionalized in Jack Kerouac's *On the Road* where Carolyn was called "Camille." She was called "Evelyn" in subsequent Kerouac novels and her actual name was used in *Some of the Dharma*. Carolyn Cassady, not only a companion to the inspiration of the Beat Generation, but a talented writer and artist in her own right, remains an important eye witness to the early Beat scene and has written a number of authoritative works on the Beat Generation. Her books include *Heart Beat: My Life With Jack and Neal* (Creative Arts Book Co., 1976)—which was the basis of the John Byrum film *Heart Beat* (1980), starring Nick Nolte, Sissy Spacek, John Heard—and *Off the Road: My Years With Cassady, Kerouac and Ginsberg* (Penguin, 1990). ✍ **NEAL CASSADY**, born February 8, 1926 in Salt Lake City, Utah, became the everlasting folk hero of the Beat generation through the writings of those who knew him—most notably Jack Kerouac and Allen Ginsberg. Cassady met Kerouac and Ginsberg in 1946 and became obsessed with their intellectual lifestyle. They in turn were drawn to and inspired by his life-lived-on-the-edge character and enigmatic personality. Cassady and Kerouac began a series of cross-country adventures that have become legend in Kerouac's *On The Road* (1957) where Cassady's persona was immortalized in the book's main character, Dean Moriarty. Cassady's story is known for a life lived by the suave instincts of a harmless con-artist with true adventures of stolen cars, cross-country travels, experiments with sex and drugs, and three marriages. His relationship with his wife Carolyn was the subject of the motion picture *Heart Beat* (1980), based on Carolyn Cassady's autobiography, *Heart Beat: My Life With Jack and Neal* (Creative Arts Book Co., 1976). Neal Cassady also appears as the main character in *Go* by John Clellon Holmes and *The Electric Kool-Aid Acid Test* by Tom Wolfe. Cassady died on February 4, 1968 in San Miguel de Allende, Mexico shortly after he was found comatose from drugs, alcohol and inclement weather alongside a railroad. He died four days short of his 42nd birthday. ✍ **ANDREI CODRESCU** is a poet, novelist, and essayist, whose many books include the novel *Wakefield* (Algonquin, 2004); *It Was Today: New Poems* (2003); *Casanova in Bohemia* (2002); *Ay, Cuba: a Socio-Erotic Journey* (2001); *Messiah* (1999); *The Blood Countess* (1996); and *Alien Candor: Selected Poems, 1970-1995*. Codrescu is also a regular commentator on National Public Radio and has written and starred in the Peabody Award-winning movie, *Road Scholar*. He is MacCurdy Distinguished Professor of English and Comparative Literature at Louisiana State University in Baton Rouge, Louisiana, where he edits *Exquisite Corpse: a Journal of Letters & Life* (www.exquisitecorpse.org). ✍ **LEONARD COHEN** (www.leonardcohenfiles.com), born to a middle-class Jewish-Canadian family on September 21, 1934 in Montréal, Canada, has enjoyed a widely successful writing career as a poet, novelist and songwriter. Cohen's first collection of poetry, *Let Us Compare Mythologies*, was published in 1956 and he came to international acclaim in 1961 with his second collection, *The Spice Box of Earth*. Subsequent works include the 1964 controversial collection *Flowers for Hitler* and two novels, *The Favorite Game* (1963) and *Beautiful Loser* (1966), which he wrote while living in Greece. He then focused his talents toward a musical career, for which he is probably best known; starting with a remarkable début with "Suzanne" championed by Judy Collins. Other early hits securing his acclaim as a songwriter include "Hey That's No Way To Say Goodbye," "So Long Marianne," and "Sisters of Mercy." Cohen has released some fourteen albums and various musical compilations over the years, including his biggest commercial success *I'm Your Man* (1988). More recently, during the 1990s and 2000s, while living in California, Cohen has continued his creative output: releasing albums and publishing *Stranger Music*, the most complete text available of his poetry and songs. After spending much of the 1990s at the Zen Center of Mount Baldy, California, Leonard Cohen now lives and works in Los Angeles. He continues to write and release new albums—his stunning *Dear Heather* was released in October, 2004—and a collection of his previously unpublished poetry is currently being prepared for publication. ✍ **BILLY COLLINS**'s latest collection of poetry is *Nine Horses* (Random House, 2002). He is the editor of *Poetry 180: A Turning Back to Poetry*. He served as United States Poet Laureate (2001-2003) and is currently New York State Poet Laureate (2004-2006). He is a Distinguished Professor at the City University of New York. ✍ **CAITLIN CONDELL** is currently a student at Oberlin College. She lives in New York City. ✍ **HOLLY CRAWFORD** is a cross media artist, poet, contemporary art historian (www.art-poetry.info) and publisher of *AC (Art Circles)*. Crawford's work pushes genre lines as she plays with paint, words, punctuation and found material. Work includes performance-participation installations *13 Ways Of Looking at a Blackbird* (Florence, 2002; Berlin, 2004; Valencia, 2005; Beijing, 2005), *Open Adoption for Art*, and an art, poetry and criticism project called *Voice Over* that is published in *NY Arts Magazine*. Crawford was born in California and now resides in New York. ✍ **VICTOR HERNÁNDEZ CRUZ** was born in 1949 in Aguas Buenas, Puerto Rico. He immigrated to the United States in 1954 and attended high school in New York. In the 1970s, Cruz emerged as a distinctive voice in the so-called Nuyorican school of émigré poets. He is the author of numerous collections of poetry, among them *Maraca: New and Selected Poems 1965-2000* (Coffee House Press, 2001), *Panaramas* (1997), *Red Beans* (1991), and *Tropicalization* (1976). Cruz is a co-founder of both the East Harlem Gut Theatre in New York and the Before Columbus Foundation. His honors include a Guggenheim award, a fellowship from The National Endowment for the Arts, and a New York Poetry Foundation award. Cruz divides his time between Puerto Rico and New York. ✍ **DAVE CUNLIFFE**, British Beat poet and editor of the underground *Global Tapestry Journal*, lives in Blackburn, Lancashire, U.K., where, he says, he enters geriatric meltdown and organic decrepitude with enthusiasm. His two companions (Rena and Mister Kryton) provide structural order and safe foundation. Hermetic solitude and global postal communication. Primitive gardening methodology and technological computerised innovation. All opposites fused and interconnected into a rustic tantric chaos. He continues to write for prankster and literary magazines on the inner and outer edges of creativity. ✍ **TONY CURTIS**, born in 1946 in Carmarthen, west Wales, is Professor of Poetry at the University of Glamorgan where he directs the M.Phil. in Writing. He has published over twenty books of poetry, criticism and cultural commentary. His ninth collection of poetry *Heaven's Gate* was published four years ago by Seren Books. They'll re-publish *Welsh Painters Talking* and the anthology *Love from Wales* again in 2005. Professor Curtis resides in Barry, Wales. ✍ **JEN DALTON** (jendalton.com) struggles with self-definition; but tends towards poetry, writing-for-hire (and her mortgage), collage art and many ephemeral follies. She was raised by Midwestern howler monkeys and eventually migrated to San Francisco where she has had the pleasure of studying poetics with Diane di Prima. ✍ **ANDREW DARLINGTON** has been interviewing Rock's luminaries and legends for several decades—spurred on as a child in the late-sixties by testosterone, the napalm that was Elvis, and hopes to bed hippie chicks. A regular contributor to *Hot Press*, *Rock'n'Reel*, *Jamming*, *Zig Zag*, *Terminal*, *International Times*, *Headpress*, and *Global Tapestry Journal*, Darlington's early collection *Slits in Aerosol Green* was reviewed by *New Musical Express* as "poetry from a twisted mind." He later proposed marriage to Jefferson Airplane Ice Queen Grace Slick (during an interview), and she didn't actually turn him down. The full story appears in his book, *I Was Elvis Presley's Bastard Love-Child* (Headpress, 2001). Darlington lives in Yorkshire, Great Britain. ✍ **JAMES DEAN**, born James Byron Dean on February 8, 1931 in Marion, Indiana, is part of an American pop culture "trinity", which also includes Marilyn Monroe and Elvis Presley. Dean starred in only three major films during his short but brilliant career: Elia Kazan's production of John Steinbeck's *East of Eden* (1955); Nicholas Ray's *Rebel Without a Cause* (1955)—in which Dean became one of cinema's greatest cultural icons, epitomizing the rebellion of 1950s teens—and George Stevens' film of Edna Ferber's *Giant*, which was just coming to a close when, ironically, Dean filmed a public service spot on auto safety before being killed in a road accident (in his new Porsche 550 Spyder) on September 30, 1955 in Cholame, California. Just two hours before the accident, he had received a speeding ticket. His death set off a world-wide wave of cultist mourning unequaled since the death of Rudolph Valentino. James Dean, the only actor in history to receive more than one Academy Award nomination posthumously, is buried in Park Cemetery in his home town of Fairmount, Indiana. ✍ **ALBERT FLYNN DESILVER** is the author of books and chapbooks including *Walking Tooth & Cloud* (2000), *Some Nature* (2001), and *Letters to Early Street*, which has been a finalist for the Four Way Books Levis Poetry Prize 2003. DeSilver has published poems in numerous literary journals, and his visual work has been shown at The Armand Hammer Museum, Los Angeles; Westmont College, Santa Barbara; and New Langton Arts, San Francisco. He is also editor/publisher of The Owl Press (www.theowlpress.com), publishing innovative poetry and poetic collaborations. He lives in Forest Knolls, California. ✍ **PETER JAMES DREW** was born in Plymouth, Massachusetts. He studied in West Virginia for two years before he received a dual Bachelors degree from the University of Massachusetts. He now lives just outside Boulder, Colorado and recently received his Master in Poetics from Naropa University. He is coeditor of *Sliding Uteri: A Rebirth of Poetic Language*. ✍ **JORDAN ESSOE** is a writer and visual artist living in San Francisco. He studied at the San Francisco Art Institute and the Pacific Northwest College of Art. He has been awarded scholarships from the La Quinta Arts Foundation, the Leta Kennedy Foundation, the San Francisco Art Institute, and the Pacific Northwest College of Art. In 2001, he was Artist-in-Residence at the Palm Springs Desert Museum. His installation *Picture Frames* was exhibited at the Palm Springs Desert Museum in 2003. He has written art criticism for the online magazine *Stretcher* (www.stretcher.org). His video poetry work has been shown internationally, most recently at the 2004 Zebra Poetry Film Award Festival, in Berlin. ✍ **LAWRENCE FERLINGHETTI** was an integral part of the Beat movement, both as a bookseller and publisher of City Lights Press. A longtime resident of San Francisco, he has served as that city's first poet laureate. He is the author of numerous books, including *A Coney Island of the Mind*, which has sold nearly a million copies. Ferlinghetti is a member of the American Academy of Arts & Letters. ✍ **MARILYN YVONNE FORD**, aka Fresno massage parlor owner Marilyn Laird, born on a farm in Austin, Indiana, has spent most of her life in California. While operating her massage businesses, Ford not only began writing but went to real estate school; becoming a licensed Realtor then, after moving to Fountain Valley, California, earning her broker's license to become a successful real estate broker. While a broker, she began taking classes at California State University of Long Beach and from there, in 1983, earned her degree in Psychology, with a minor in Sociology. In 1992, Ford returned to Fresno, California, to host a popular radio talk show called *Moments with Marilyn*. She's also been the subject of numerous newspaper articles in *The Fresno Bee*, and did a television commercial for Fresno's Paul's Auto Sales. Ford's since become an eclectic artist who paints and, inspired by the works of Marcel Duchamp, takes everyday objects and turns them into works of art. Currently writing her first book of poems, entitled *Passing Shadows*, Marilyn Ford, the mother of four children, lives in Fresno, California. ✍ **GLORIA FRYM** is a poet and fiction writer. Her last book of poems,

Homeless At Home, won an American Book Award in 2002. She is the author of two critically acclaimed collections of short stories, *Distance No Object* and *How I Learned*, as well as several volumes of poetry and articles on photography and other visual media. She is a recipient of two Fund for Poetry Awards, the Walter & Elise Haas Creative Work Fund Grant, and the San Francisco State University Poetry Center Book Award. She teaches at California College of the Arts, and recently served as Distinguished Writer in Residence at St. Mary's College in Moraga, California. ✍ **TESS GALLAGHER**, a poet, essayist, novelist, translator and screenwriter has recently completed work on a poetry manuscript entitled: *Dear Ghosts,* (the comma is a part of the title) and in Spring 2004 she received an Honorary Doctorate from Hartford University and a Lifetime Achievement Award from the Washington State Poets Association. In Fall 2004 she helped her Irish companion Josie Gray with showings of his paintings in America and at Kennys Bookshop and Art Gallery in Galway, Ireland (http://search.kennys.ie). As the widow of internationally known short story writer Raymond Carver, she continues to be involved daily in all that pertains to his work, the latest event being a boxed set of the film *Short Cuts* with various documentaries and the stories used in the film directed by Robert Altman. She lives in Port Angeles, Washington, on the Olympic Peninsula in Sky House. Her poems here included in volume 4 of *Van Gogh's Ear* will appear in *Dear Ghosts,* which will be published by Graywolf Press in April of 2006. ✍ **MARCENE GANDOLFO**'s poems have appeared recently in *The Paterson Literary Review, Earth's Daughters, Squaw Valley Review* and *Poetry Evolution*. She has taught writing at several northern California colleges and currently lives in Elk Grove, California. ✍ **JOHN GILMORE** (www.johngilmore.com) began his fascinating life as a child actor, then went on to become a stage and motion picture player; poet (published infrequently since the 1960s); playwright; screenwriter; B-movie director; true-crime writer and novelist. Gilmore's books include *Live Fast, Die Young: Remembering The Short Life of James Dean*; *Severed: The True Story of the Black Dahlia Murder*; *Manson: The Unholy Trail of Charlie and the Family*; and *Laid Bare: A Memoir of Wrecked Lives and the Hollywood Death Trip*. William S. Burroughs praised Gilmore's controversial novel, *Fetish Blonde*. Recently featured in the book, *Star Culture* (Phaidon), Gilmore has two books being released this Spring, a nonfiction: *L.A. Despair: A Landscape of Crimes & Bad Times*; and a novel, *Crazy Streak* (Scapegoat Publishing). He is currently working on a second book of memoirs, *Sex, Death & The Hollywood Mystique*; and a book of poetry. ✍ **JOHN GIORNO**, born December 4, 1936 in New York City, is considered the originator of performance poetry, as well as one of the most innovative and influential figures of 20th century poetry. A stockbroker turned poet, Giorno met Andy Warhol at Eleanor Ward's Stable Gallery in November 1962 and, soon after becoming friends, briefly indulged Warhol's foot fetish. On Memorial Day weekend in 1963 they went away for a few days and Giorno woke up in the night to find Warhol staring at him—Warhol took a lot of speed in those days. "Would you like to be a movie star?" asked Warhol. "Of course," said Giorno, "I want to be just like Marilyn Monroe." Thus John Giorno became Andy Warhol's first superstar; starring in Warhol's first film, *Sleep* (1963), in which Giorno was filmed sleeping. In 1968, Giorno created Dial-A-Poem, making use of the telephone for the first time to communicate to mass audiences. Known for his bold, graphic subject matter, he has released numerous recordings and published over twenty books including, *Balling Buddha* (1970), *Grasping at Emptiness* (1985), and *Just Say No To Family Values* (2000). Giorno's memoir, *You Got To Burn To Shine* (Serpent's Tail, 1994) details his relationships with Andy Warhol and Keith Haring, his experience as a Tibetan Buddhist and his understanding of death in the age of AIDS. For many years Giorno performed with William Burroughs and with The John Giorno Band (1984-89). Giorno's poem "Everyone Gets Lighter", here included in volume 4 of *Van Gogh's Ear*, was posted as a billboard on Staten Island for six months in September 2003. ✍ **DAVID HELWIG** (www.davidhelwig.com), born in Toronto on April 15, 1938, has published thirteen volumes of poetry. Following the publication of his first collection, *Figures in a Landscape* (1967), Margaret Atwood referred to his "astonishing range and versatility." Helwig's most recent volume is a long poem, *The Year One* (Gaspereau Press, 2004), which he considers "both a new departure and a summing up." Helwig has also had novels appear with various publishers including Viking Penguin. He now lives in a village in Canada's smallest province, Prince Edward Island. ✍ **JILL HILL**'s background has many colours—as actress, painter, community nurse, university lecturer and school teacher, and with a number of degrees including a Bachelor of Creative Arts and Master of Science. Jill Hill has traveled very broadly around the world and lived in Asia for the last 9 years—through peaceful and violent times, and where many of her strongest understandings of alternative lives and cultures have been forged. Poetry is a new passion—primarily a means of self-exploration; the poems in this fourth volume of *Van Gogh's Ear* represent her début. ✍ **MARIE HOUZELLE** grew up in the south of France and now lives in Ivry near Paris. On and off over the last few years she has co-edited the literary magazine *Pharos*. Houzelle's chapbook *No Sex Last Noon* (I Want Press) came out in 2000. A novel she finished last year is looking for a title (and a publisher). Houzelle is currently writing another novel and more poetry. ✍ **SCOTT HUTCHISON** (www.scotthutchison.com), born in Indianola, Iowa in April 1973, became interested in art at a very early age when he saw Francis Bacon's painting *Study after Velásquez's Portrait of Pope Innocent X*. This haunting image of a screaming pope with rich purples and blacks streaming down the surface—its mood and its power—still drives Hutchison to create his images. After receiving his BFA in painting from Drake University (Des Moines, IA) in 1992, he subsequently pursued a year of independent painting and study in Bath, England. He received his MFA from George Washington University in 1999, and has continued painting in his Arlington, Virginia studio. An exploration of the human figure through paint continues to be the leitmotiv of his work. For several years, Hutchison's figures existed in surreal settings, embedded in colorless landscapes. More recently, color has crept back into his paintings, and a long-standing interest in animation has become part of his creative process. Scott Hutchison has exhibited his work extensively throughout the Washington metropolitan area, including numerous solo exhibitions. Most recently, in the Fall of 2003, his large-scale nude paintings attracted the attention of NBC, where his work was covered in a news feature. ✍ **MICHAEL HUXLEY**, editorial director of STARbooks Press (www.starbookspress.com), has compiled four anthologies of literotica: *Fantasies Made Flesh*; *Saints and Sinners*; *Men, Amplified*; and *Wet Nightmares, Wet Dreams*. His most recent work appears in *Friction 7*; *Best Gay Love Stories 2005*; *Best Gay Erotica 2005*; *I Do, I Don't: Queers on Marriage*; and *Walking Higher: Gay Men Write About the Death of Their Mothers*. ✍ **BRENDAN KENNELLY**, born in 1936 in Ballylongford, Co. Kerry, was educated at St. Ita's college in Tarbert, Co. Kerry and later at Trinity College, Dublin where he has been professor of Modern Literature since 1975. Kennelly is one of Ireland's most important contemporary poets whose prolific output extends to over forty volumes of poetry since the publication of his first poetic work in 1959. His seminal, critically acclaimed collections include *Cromwell* (1983), *The Book of Judas* (1991), *Poetry My Arse* (1995) and *The Man Made of Rain* (1998). He is also a celebrated dramatist, novelist, editor and anthologist. A landmark volume of Brendan Kennelly's poetry, *Familiar Strangers: New & Selected Poems 1960-2004* has recently been released by Bloodaxe Books. ✍ **GALWAY KINNELL** was born in Providence, Rhode Island, in 1927. He studied at Princeton University and the University of Rochester. His volumes of poetry include *A New Selected Poems* (Houghton Mifflin, 2000), a finalist for the National Book Award; *Imperfect Thirst* (1996); *When One Has Lived a Long Time Alone* (1990); *Selected Poems* (1980), for which he received both the Pulitzer Prize and the National Book Award; *Mortal Acts, Mortal Words* (1980); *The Book of Nightmares* (1971); *Body Rags* (1968); *Flower Herding on Mount Monadnock* (1964); and *What a Kingdom It Was* (1960). He has also published translations of works by Yves Bonnefroy, Yvanne Goll, François Villon, and Rainer Maria Rilke. Galway Kinnell divides his time between Vermont and New York City, where he is the Erich Maria Remarque Professor of Creative Writing at New York University. He is currently a Chancellor of The Academy of American Poets. ✍ **RICHARD KOSTELANETZ** (www.richardkostelanetz.com) is a prolific author, critic, editor, and artist. Since the 1960s he has written and edited close to one hundred books. His essays, poems, fictions, and experimental prose explore the limits of language. An esteemed avant-garde author, he has also worked with various other media, including audio recordings, holograms, photographs, video and film, prints, and high-tech installations. Individual entries on Richard Kostelanetz appear in: *Contemporary Poets*; *Contemporary Novelists*; *Postmodern Fiction*; *Baker's Biographical Dictionary of Musicians*; *A Reader's Guide to Twentieth-Century Writers*; the *Merriam-Webster Encyclopedia of Literature*; *Webster's Dictionary of American Authors*; *The HarperCollins Reader's Encyclopedia of American Literature*; and the *Encyclopedia Britannica*, among other distinguished directories. Living in New York, where he was born, he still needs two bucks to take a subway. ✍ **RICHARD KRECH** was born in 1946. In 1966 he started a poetry magazine, *Avalanche*, and sponsored open poetry readings at a bookstore on Telegraph Avenue in Berkeley, California for several years. His first chapbook was published by D. A. Levy in Cleveland. Krech had several other small books of poetry published, as well as work published in numerous poetry magazines. In 1976, Krech started law school and has been practicing criminal defense in Oakland, California since 1980. In 2001, after a 25+ year line break, he began writing poetry again and has had two chapbooks published and more poems appear in several magazines. His poem "Premeditated, Deliberated & Intentional", here in

Van Gogh's Ear 4, is from a work-in-progress on criminal defense practice entitled *The Bodhisattva of the Public Defender's Office*. ✍ **JOANNE KYGER** is a California poet, with ties to the San Francisco Renaissance and the Beat Generation. The winner of the National Poetry Series in 1983 for her book, *Going On* (E. P. Dutton), Kyger has published numerous volumes of poetry, the most recent being, *As Ever: Selected Poems* (Penguin, 2002). She teaches at Naropa University's writing program, the New College of San Francisco, and now also at Mills College in Oakland. ✍ **J. T. LEROY** (www.jtleroy.com) is the author of international best sellers, *The Heart Is Deceitful Above All Things* (now a film, directed by and starring Asia Argento, which recently premiered at Cannes), and *Sarah* (being made into a film by Steven Shainberg). His third novel will be released by Viking in 2005. A novella, *Harold's End* (Last Gasp, 2005), with illustrations by Cherry Hood, has just been released. J. T. LeRoy is Associate Producer on Gus Van Sant's film, *Elephant*, winner of the Palme d'Or at Cannes. He has begun another collaborative project with Van Sant and is currently writing its original screenplay. He is also writing and producing a short film for Palm Pictures, around the band Earlimart. He is part of the rock band, Thistle (www.thistlehq.com), who are recording their debut with producer Jerry Harrison. LeRoy is a contributing editor for *Index*, *Flaunt*, *7x7*, *i-D* as well as writes for *Spin*, *GQ*, *Sunday London Times*, etc. J. T. both treasures and appreciates gifts of very dark chocolate and Hot Wheels cars. ✍ **LYN LIFSHIN** (www.lynlifshin.com) is an icon of the contemporary American poetry scene. Her recent prizewinning book (Paterson Poetry Award), *Before It's Light*, was published winter 1999-2000 by Black Sparrow press, following their publication of *Cold Comfort* in 1997. *Another Woman Who Looks Like Me* will be published in 2005 by Black Sparrow-David Godine (www.blacksparrowbooks.com). Also recently published is *A New Film About a Woman in Love with the Dead* (March Street Press). She has published more than 100 books of poetry, won awards for her non-fiction and edited 4 anthologies of women's writing. Her poems have appeared in most literary and poetry magazines and she is the subject of an award-winning documentary film, *Lyn Lifshin: Not Made of Glass*, available from Women Make Movies. An update to her Gale Research Projects Autobiographical series, "On The Outside, Lips, Blues, Blue Lace," was published Spring 2003. She is working on a collection of poems about the famous, short lived beautiful race horse, Ruffian: *The Licorice Daughter: My Year with Ruffian*. New chapbooks include *When a Cat Dies* and *Another Woman's Story*. Forthcoming chapbooks include *Mad Girl Poems*, *Barbie Poems*, and *The Daughter I Don't Have*. ✍ **MARK LIPMAN** is a multi-media artist who began his career as a professional ballet dancer, working with the Kirov Ballet of Saint Petersburg; the Royal Danish Ballet of Copenhagen; the Houston Ballet; and, among others, the Ballet Theatre of Boston. After settling in Paris in 1996, Lipman turned toward writing and published his first novel, *Impermanence*, in 2001, which was then nominated for the Bard Literary Prize in 2002. In the same year, he had the opportunity to work with Lawrence Ferlinghetti, John Hirshman and the Italian poet, Igor Costanzo, in *Back to Beat*, a Fluxus art and poetry event in Breccia, Italy. In 2003, Lipman began work as a serious painter and to date has completed 40 canvasses, most of which were displayed during a six-month public exposition in Paris in 2004. His recent works include a novella,

Ignascious (2003); a book of poems, *Love and Politics* (2003); and a second novel, *Tumbleweed* (2004). ✄ **KEN MACKENZIE** is a South African-born writer living in Paris. Two novels, *A Dragon to Kill* and *The Deserter*, were published in London by Eyre and Spottiswoode. He has also published short stories, including two read on the BBC, and poetry, mostly in the Paris literary journal, *Pharos*. ✄ **JAYANTA MAHAPATRA** has read and published his poetry around the world. A physicist, he has authored sixteen collections of poetry in English and five in his native Oriya. His new volume of poetry should appear in 2005. He lives in Cuttack in Orissa, India, where he edits the literary journal, *Chandrabhágá*. ✄ **NORMAN MAILER** (www.iol.ie/~kic), born January 31, 1923 in Long Branch, New Jersey, was brought up in Brooklyn, and went to Harvard when he was sixteen. Mailer achieved fame with the publication of his World War II novel, *The Naked and The Dead* (1948), which was based on his own experiences serving in the Pacific. A prolific writer, Mailer's many books include: *The Deer Park* (1955), which has been adapted into a play and was successfully produced off Broadway; *Why Are We in Vietnam?* (1967), which was nominated for a National Book Award; *Armies of the Night* (1968) which won both the Pulitzer Prize and the National Book Award, and brought Mailer both popular and critical acclaim; *Miami and the Siege of Chicago* (1968), which won a National Book Award for nonfiction; *Of a Fire on the Moon* (1970); *The Prisoner of Sex* (1971); *Marilyn* (1973); *The Executioner's Song* (1979), winning Mailer his second Pulitzer Prize, and nominated for the American Book Award and National Book Critics Circle Award (Mailer also wrote the script for the film version of *The Executioner's Song* and received an Emmy nomination for best adaptation); and *Harlot's Ghost* (1991). Mailer's other credits include writing, directing and appearing in a number of motion pictures. ✄ **RANDALL MANN**, born in Provo, Utah, was raised in Kentucky and Florida. He was educated at the University of Florida, and is the author of *Complaint in the Garden* (Zoo Press, 2004), winner of the 2003 Kenyon Review Prize in Poetry. Mann's poems and reviews have appeared in the *Kenyon Review, New Republic, Paris Review, Poetry, Salmagundi*, and *Verse*. He lives in San Francisco. ✄ **SYLVIA MILES** is still a force of nature. Nominated for two Academy Awards for *Midnight Cowboy* (1970) and *Farewell My Lovely* (1976), New York's own Sylvia Miles has been a member of the Actor's Studio since 1968. Winning best actress plaudits throughout the world for Warhol's *Heat*, directed by Paul Morrisey, Ms. Miles went on to co-star with Richard Chamberlain and Dorothy McGuire in Tennessee Williams' *Night of the Iguana* at the uptown Circle in the Square, and as a result was nominated at London's Piccadilly Theatre as "Actress of the Year" for Tennessee Williams' "Vieux Carré." Ms. Miles has gone on to make over 30 films, among them Tom McGuane's *Ninety-Two In The Shade*; Tobe Hooper's *Funhouse*; *The Sentinel*; *Crossing Delancey*; *Wall Street*; and *She-Devil*. Presently a documentary is being made on her life by Merchant Films. ✄ **LAURE MILLET**'s stories and poems have been published in the Paris-based magazines *Gare du Nord*, *Pharos*, and *Upstairs at Duroc*; and in the U.S. in *Skanky Possum* and *Blue Book Poetry*. She lives in Paris. ✄ Freedom fighter **TASLIMA NASRIN / NASREEN** (taslimanasrin.com), born August 25, 1962 in Mymensingh, Bangladesh, comes from a very conservative Muslim background. After the huge success of her second poetry book in 1989, she started writing regular columns in progressive newspapers and publishing best-selling books translated in 20 languages. Her criticism of Islam and the oppressive customs that discriminate against women caused fundamentalist organization to issue a fatwa against her, a price was set on her head. According to her, the religious scriptures are out of time and out of place, women should receive equality and justice. Her views led fourteen different political and non-political organizations to unite for the first time, starting violent demonstrations, calling a general strike, blocking government offices, and demanding her immediate execution by hanging. After escaping confinement and assaults by fundamentalist mobs, she exiled in Europe. Her 28 books of poetry, essays, and novels have received numerous awards in Western countries. In Bangladesh, they are banned. Her own government forbade her to return. In 1998, she risked a last trip to be with her ailing mother but was forced to leave. When her mother died, no Imam came to lead her funeral, her crime being that she was the mother of an infidel.

✍ **THOM NICKELS**, a Philadelphia-based author/journalist/poet and film critic, is the author of *The Cliffs of Aries* (1988), *Walking Water & After All This* (1989), *The Boy on the Bicycle* (1993–94), *Manayunk* (2001), *Gay and Lesbian Philadelphia* (2002–03), and *Tropic of Libra* (2003). Nickels has written commentary pieces, celebrity interviews, features and book reviews for local and national publications, including *The Gay and Lesbian Worldwide Review* and is a Contributing Editor for Philadelphia's *Weekly Press*. Nickels will write *Revelations: The History of Gay and Lesbian Philadelphia*, a documentary film on his book, *Gay and Lesbian Philadelphia* (Longshore Films, Inc.). His new book, *Out in History*, will be published by the Florida Literary Foundation sometime in early 2005. ✍ **ALICE NOTLEY**, born November 8, 1945, married the writer Ted Berrigan in 1972, with whom she had two sons. After Berrigan's death in 1983, she married the British poet Douglas Oliver and relocated to Paris, France, where she now lives permanently. Notley has published more than twenty books, including: *Selected Poems of Alice Notley* (Talisman, 1993); *The Descent of Alette* (Penguin, 1996); *Mysteries of Small Houses* (Penguin, 1998), which was one of three nominees for the Pulitzer Prize and the winner of the Los Angeles Times Book Award for Poetry; *Disobedience* (Penguin, 2001); and most recently The Owl Press (www.theowlpress.com) published chapbook, *From the Beginning* (2004). In April 2001, Alice Notley received The Shelley Memorial Award from the Poetry Society of America, and in May 2001 she received an award in literature from the American Academy of Arts and Letters. *Coming After*, her book of essays on poets and poetry, is due out from University of Michigan Press in 2005. With her sons, Anselm Berrigan and Edmund Berrigan, Notley has been editing *The Collected Poems of Ted Berrigan*, which will be published by the University of California Press in 2005. ✍ **JOYCE CAROL OATES**, born June 16, 1938 in Lockport, New York, is a recipient of the National Book Award, the PEN/Malamud Award for Excellence in Short Fiction, and the Bram Stoker Award from the Horror Writers of America. She has written some of the most enduring fiction of our time, including: *Broke Heart Blues*; *Black Water*; *Because It Is Bitter, Because It Is My Heart*; and the national bestsellers *We Were the Mulvaneys* (Plume, 1996) and *Blonde: A Novel* (Ecco, 2000), the latter nominated for the National Book Award. Oates is the Roger S. Berlind Distinguished Professor of Humanities at

Princeton University and has been a member since 1978 of the American Academy of Arts and Letters. A prolific writer, Joyce Carol Oates has published a number of recent and forthcoming books, including: *I Am No One You Know: Stories* (Ecco, 2004); *The Falls: A Novel*; (Ecco, 2004); *Sexy* (Harper Tempest, 2005); and *Uncensored: Views & (Re)views* (Ecco, 2005). She lives in Princeton, New Jersey. ✍ **TOMMY FRANK O'CONNOR** is a poet, novelist and story writer living in Tralee, Co. Kerry, Ireland. His published works include: *The Poacher's Apprentice* (Marino Books, 1997); *Kee Kee, Cup & Tok* (Wynkin de Worde, 2004); *Loose Head* (Doghouse, 2004). *Attic Warpipes*—a collection of poetry—is due from Bradshaw Books in January 2005. He performs his work at many literary festivals, and facilitates workshops with writers of all ages. ✍ **NESSA O'MAHONY** was born in Dublin in 1964. Her poetry has appeared in a number of Irish, UK and North American periodicals including: *Poetry Ireland Review*; *The Shop*; *Fortnight*; *The Sunday Tribune*; *InCognito*; *The Stinging Fly*; *Agenda*; *Books Ireland*; *In Media Res* (Canada); *Iota*; and the *Atlanta Review*. O'Mahony has also been broadcast by Irish state radio. Her first poetry collection, entitled *Bar Talk*, was published by iTaLiCs Press in Dublin in 1999. Her second, *Trapping a Ghost*, will be published by Bluechrome Publishing (www.bluechrome.co.uk) in Spring 2005. She was recently awarded an Irish Arts Council literature bursary and edits the online literary magazine, *Electric Acorn* (http://acorn.dublinwriters.org). O'Mahony is currently undertaking a PhD in Creative Writing at the University of Wales, Bangor. ✍ **YOKO ONO** (www.a-i-u.net), born February 18, 1933 in Tokyo, is a pioneering avant-garde artist, poet, and composer who has worked alternatively at the fringe and in the mainstream of culture for more than forty years. Her early scores and instructions established the primacy of concept, language, and participation that was central to such international art movements as Fluxus and Conceptual Art. With John Lennon, she produced numerous films, recordings, and mass-media campaigns for world peace. Yoko Ono (whose first name translates to "ocean child") continues to be an innovative and provocative force in the New York, Tokyo, and London vanguards. Her long career is linked by her profound intent to seek and provoke questions, and to engage us in that search. Yoko Ono, at the age of 71, has spectacularly topped the American dance chart with her track, called *Every Man Has A Man Who Loves Him*, a revamped version of her 1980s hit *Every Man Has A Woman Who Loves Him*—this time attacking American President George W. Bush for banning gay marriage. ✍ **LISA PASOLD** is a poet and freelance journalist who writes about travel, architecture and culture. She's been thrown off a train in Belarus, been fed the world's best pigeon pie in Marrakech, has mushed huskies in the Yukon, and been cheated in the Venetian gambling halls of Ca' Vendramin Calergi. Pasold grew up in Montréal and currently lives in Paris. Her new book of poetry, *Weave* (2004), was published by Frontenac House (www.frontenachouse.com). ✍ **BARBARA PHILIPP** (www.barbaraphilipp.com) was born in Graz (Austria) on 15 April 1977. In 1995, Philipp passed the examination for the Academy of Fine Arts in Vienna, and two years later was accepted as a student at the Academy of Fine Arts in Paris, where she earned her degree in 2002. Awarded a scholarship in 2001 from the Städelschule in Frankfurt am Main, Germany, she went there for a year to study with Hermann Nitsch. In 2004, Philipp earned her degree in

Vienna where she participated in several workshops, including those of Joan Jonas and Erwin Wurm; not to mention an animation film program with T. Renoldner. In Frankfurt, she became interested in "live action" performances—often related to food and nutrition—where the public is invited to take an active role. Her most recent "live action" performance, titled *Thanksgiving*, took place on 25 November 2004 in Vienna's former slaughterhouse. Philipp currently divides her time between Vienna (Austria) and Amsterdam (Netherlands). ✍ **KRISTIN PREVALLET** is the author of *Scratch Sides: Poetry*; *Documentation*; and *Image-Text Projects* (2002). She lives in Brooklyn, New York. ✍ **DIANE Di PRIMA** is almighty sick of writing bios and can no longer distinguish the banality of her "real life" from the various lies she has learned by rote from her siblings, critics, and others. This year she turned seventy on three or four different occasions, and is fairly sure she isn't a kangaroo. The pestiferous urge to shout the titles of her unborn books from rooftops has long since dispersed like jelly donuts foolishly baked in an alchemist's oven. ✍ **TERRY RENTZEPIS** (www.alltenthumbs.com), at the urgings of his wife, picked up a paint brush and began painting to fight the long, lonely, painful hours of recovery after undergoing major back surgery. A self-taught, lifetime doodler, Rentzepis grew into a successful artist who, working in acrylic, creates morphed characters with an emotional impact that makes one feel as if they've caught each character in the most intense of private moments. He's recently completed his first gallery show in Miami, Florida. His work has been published in: *Fifteen Project*; *Retort Magazine*; *Poetic Inhalation*; and *Razorcake Magazine*. Rentzepis lives in Coconut Grove, Florida, with his beautiful wife, Sheri, and their five-month-old son, Jake; not to mention a Doberman named "Ghost", a min-pin named "Face", and a mouthy cat named "Ghetto". ✍ **BOB ROSENTHAL** is a poet and a writer. He has co-written and produced five plays. His 1970's *Cleaning Up New York* became a cult classic. His latest collection of poetry is *Viburnum*, published by White Fields Press. Having taught workshops at The Poetry Project, Snug Harbor, and Naropa Institute, he is an adjunct professor of English at New York Technical College. He worked as Allen Ginsberg's secretary for the poet's last 20 years; now serves as a trustee of the Allen Ginsberg Trust; and is currently writing his account on the business of Ginsberg. ✍ **BARNEY ROSSET**, born May 28, 1922 in Chicago, Illinois, became one of the most renowned figures in American publishing; founding Grove Press in New York City in 1951 and turning it into the most influential alternative book press of its time. Rosset's *Evergreen Review* (1957-1973) championed a generation of radicals and free thinkers with its liberal activism and erotica. Rosset published such notable French avant-garde writers as Alain Robbe-Grillet, Jean Genet, and Eugene Ionesco; American 1950s "Beat" writers Jack Kerouac, William Burroughs, and Allen Ginsberg; and key radical thinkers of the 1960s including Malcolm X, Frantz Fanon and Regis Debray. Rosset published Samuel Beckett's *Waiting for Godot* and introduced Japanese author Kenzaburo Oé to an American public. Through his legendary legal victories on the rights of free speech, Rosset also published the first unexpurgated edition of D. H. Lawrence's *Lady Chatterly's Lover* and released in America the sexually explicit Swedish documentary *I am Curious (Yellow)*. In 1988, Grove Press and *Evergreen Review* were awarded the PEN Publisher's Citation for fostering "the freedom and dignity of artists." In 1999, the French Ministry of Culture bestowed upon Rosset the honor of Commandeur dans l'Ordre des Arts et Lettres. Rosset is editor-in-chief of *Evergreen Review Online* (www.evergreenreview.com) and is currently working on his autobiography. He lives in New York City. ✍ **MICHAEL ROTHENBERG**, born in Miami Beach, Florida in 1951, is a poet and songwriter. He has been an active environmentalist in the San Francisco Bay Area for the past 25 years, where he cultivates orchids and bromeliads at his nursery, Shelldance. His songs have appeared in the films: *Shadowhunter*; *Black Day Blue Night*; and *Outside Ozona*. He is also editor and co-founder of Big Bridge Press and the online magazine, *Big Bridge* (www.bigbridge.org). Rothenberg's books of poems include: *Favorite Songs, Nightmare of the Violins* (Twowindows Press); *Man/Women*, with Joanne Kyger (Big Bridge Press); *The Paris Journals* (Fish Drum); *Grown Up Cuba* (Il Begatto Press, Amsterdam); and *Unhurried Visions* (La Alameda Press, 2003). He is also author of the novel, *Punk Rockwell* (Tropical Press, 2001). Editorial projects include: *Overtime: Selected Poems* by Philip Whalen (Penguin Putnam, Inc., 2002); *As Ever: Selected Poems* by Joanne Kyger (Penguin Books); and *David's Copy: Selected Poems of David Meltzer* (Penguin, 2004). Rothenberg divides his time between Pacifica, California and Miami, Florida. ✍ **CAROL RUMENS**, born 10 December 1944 in Forest Hill, South London, has published twelve volumes of poetry. Her most recent are *Hex* (Bloodaxe, 2002) and a collection, bringing together earlier and new work, *Poems 1968-2004* (Bloodaxe, 2004). She has won various awards, including the Alice Hunt Bartlett Prize (with Thomas McCarthy), a Cholmondeley Award and a Prudence Farmar Prize. Her plays have been produced in London, Manchester and Newcastle. She has also published a novel and edited several poetry anthologies, as well as the selected poems of Elizabeth Bartlett. Her translations from the Russian (with Yuri Drobyshev) are included in several collections, including *After Pushkin* (2001) and *Selected Poems* by Yevgeny Rein (2002). Carol Rumens currently teaches Creative Writing at the University of Wales, Bangor. A member of the Society of Authors and a member of the Welsh Academy, she lives in Bangor, North Wales. ✍ **SUE RUSSELL** (www.SueRussellWrites.com), born in London, England, is an author and internationally syndicated journalist. As a journalist, she has written over 1,500 articles for respected publications worldwide including the *Daily Telegraph*, *Independent* and *Washington Post*. She's survived climbing a 50 ft. tree with Sean Connery, puffing on a stogie with Arnold Schwarzenegger, and imbibing way too many margaritas with Ringo Starr, and her wide-ranging subjects include throwaway kids, medicinal mushrooms, models, murderers and movie stars. The author of several non-fiction books, Sue Russell's biography of executed serial killer Aileen Wuornos, *Lethal Intent* (Kensington, 2002), is her first true crime book. She resides in Los Angeles. ✍ **SONIA SANCHEZ**, affectionately and deservedly known as the "Poet Laureate of the Planet," was born Wilsonia Driver on September 9, 1934, in Birmingham, Alabama. A poet, playwright, and educator, noted for her black activism, she is one of the most important writers of the Black Arts Movement; having been an influential force in political and African American literary culture for over three decades. The recipient of many honors, including the Robert Frost Medal in Poetry (2001), Sonia Sanchez lives in Philadelphia and is the author of over sixteen books including: *Does your house have lions?* (1995), which was nominated for both the NAACP Image and National Book Critics Circle Award; *Homegirls & Handgrenades* (1984), which won the 1985 American Book Award for Poetry; and *Shake Loose My Skin: New and Selected Poems* (Beacon Press, 1999). Sonia Sanchez's new ground-breaking CD, *Full Moon of Sonia*—which fuses a wide range of musical styles and underscores her contribution to poetry and performance in the 20th century—was released by VIA International Artists in December 2004 (currently available at: www.cdbaby.com). ✍ **ARAM SAROYAN** (www.aramsaroyan.com), born September 25, 1943, is an internationally known poet, novelist, biographer, memoirist and play-wright. Son and biographer of William Saroyan, Aram Saroyan grew up in a world of celebrities and geniuses. His writings soon placed him among the best known figures in the New York School of poets, and his essays and reviews helped to characterize his generation. In fact, in the late 1960s, director Mike Nichols wanted to cast Saroyan in the lead of his movie *The Graduate*, but Saroyan walked away from the part in order to focus on his writing. The recipient of two National Endowment for the Arts poetry awards (one of them for his controversial one-word poem "lighght"), his collections of poetry include *Aram Saroyan* and *Pages* (both Random House). His largest collection, *Day and Night: Bolinas Poems*, was published by Black Sparrow Press in 1999. Among Saroyan's prose books are *Last Rites*, a book about the death of his father, the playwright and short story writer William Saroyan; *The Romantic*, a novel that was a Los Angeles Times Book Review Critics' Choice selection; and the true crime Literary Guild selection *Rancho Mirage: An American Tragedy of Manners, Madness and Murder*. Aram Saroyan's play *At the Beach House* will receive its world premiere in Los Angeles in early 2005. His play *The Evening Hour* is scheduled for production at the Armenian National Theater in Yerevan in Armenian and in Moscow in Russian. His most recent books are *Artists in Trouble: New Stories* (Black Sparrow/Godine) and *Starting Out in the Sixties: Selected Essays* (Talisman). Saroyan lives in Los Angeles with his wife, the painter Gailyn Saroyan. ✍ **LARRY SAWYER** has escaped from the display case. His bathtub overflows with gardenias and his poetry and critical reviews have been published in *Jacket, Exquisite Corpse, Shampoo, The Prague Literary Review, NY Arts, Skanky Possum, Big Bridge, Tabacaria,* and elsewhere. He lives in Chicago with his wife Lina ramona Vitkauskas in an apartment that doubles as a sitcom. In his spare time he is the editor of the online literary magazine, *milk* (www.milkmag.org). ✍ **EABHAN NÍ SHUILEABHÁIN**, born in Dublin, Ireland, is a poet and editor whose work has appeared or is forth-coming in various publications, including: *Poetry Ireland Review; Orbis, Staple; The Sunday Tribune's New Irish Writing; The Shop; Poetry Scotland; Anon; Agenda; Envoi; The Frogmore Papers;* and *Borderlines*. She is currently the poetry editor of Dublin's Literary Magazine, *The Stinging Fly* (www.stingingfly.org). Shuileabháin resides in Gwynedd, Wales. ✍ **DONNY SMITH** was raised in Nebraska, but hates sports. In 2002, Smith earned a Master of Science degree in Library & Information Science from Drexel University, Philadelphia. He's the editor of the litzine, *Dwan*; history-of-zines editor of *Xerography Debt*; and co-editor of *Library Urinal*. His poems, articles, and translations have appeared in publications such as: *Art Documentation; Buttmen; Lilliput Review;* and *Sinister Wisdom*. Donny Smith is currently a library-less librarian living in southern Indiana. ✍ **MARC SMITH** (www.slampapi.com), born Marc Kelly Smith on October 3, 1949 in Chicago, singlehandedly reignited performance poetry as a popular art form by bringing to the poetry community a new style of presentation that has given birth to a literary movement known as Poetry Slam. Marrying at the age of 20, and living in South Carolina during the civil rights movement, he pursued his dream of becoming a writer. Several of life's tragedies, however, sent him and his wife back to Chicago where he followed his father's path in construction. He and his wife, Amy, raised three children: Adam, Carl and Sara, while Marc Smith rose to a comfortable position as a construction project manager. The day came in 1983 when he gave up the straight and narrow to follow his dream. He read his first poem publicly in 1984, and soon started the Monday Night Poetry Readings at the Get Me High. Evolving as a poet, Smith found a home in 1987 at the Green Mill Tavern for his own unique style of performance poetry, and Poetry Slam was born. Since then performance poetry has spread throughout the country to more than 150 American cities and each year teams compete in the National Poetry Slam. *Crowdpleaser* (Collage Press, 1996) is Smith's first published book. He has recently expanded his talents to theatrical productions in Chicago through acting and writing. ✍ **CAROLYN STOLOFF**, a native and lifelong New Yorker, poet and painter, taught both poetry and studio art at the college level. Her poems have appeared in a wide variety of publications, including: *The New Yorker*; *The Nation*; *Bomb*; *The Bitter Oleander*; and *Indiana Review*. Her ninth poetry book of poetry, *Reaching for Honey*, published by Red Hen Press in Spring 2004, is available through amazon.com. ✍ **NELSON SULLIVAN** (www.climage.ch), New York's extraordinary chronicler of the Downtown scene in the 1980s, was a genius video filmmaker who predated all of MTV in style by bringing his musical skills to his work, and creating a new cinematography. Sullivan filmed the New York gay and transvestite scene in the 1980s. He would carry the camera at arms length moving through the crowd in graceful curves. Never editing his tapes later, Sullivan would edit in-camera as he went along. He would accompany his filming with commentary, and was never too self-conscious to turn the camera on himself. The result of this combination of crew, cameraman, director, presenter and editor in a one-man band was carried off with such skill, that his footage flowed like music and was orchestrated like a concert, drawing you in and making you feel as if you really were there. When Nelson Sullivan died suddenly in 1989, his extensive trove of footage—with its many exciting personalities, such as Sylvia Miles, RuPaul, James St. James, actress Lisa Edelstein, and the incomparable Christina, made immortal by Marilyn Manson—included over 1500 hours of videotape from 1982-1989. ✍ **MARK TERRILL**, a native Californian and former merchant seaman, has lived in Germany since 1984, where he has worked as a shipyard welder, road manager for rock bands, cook and postal worker. Recent books include a collection of poems, *The United Colors of Death* (Pathwise Press, 2003); a collection of prose poems, *Bread & Fish* (The Figures, 2002); a memoir, *Here to Learn: Remembering Paul Bowles* (Green Bean Press, 2002); as well as a collection of translations, *Like a Pilot: Rolf Dieter Brinkmann, Selected Poems 1963-1970* (Sulphur River Literary Review Press, 2001). ✍ **JOHN UPDIKE**, born March 18, 1932 in Reading,

Pennsylvania, is an American novelist, short story writer, and poet. Well known for his well-crafted prose that explores the hidden tensions of middle-class American life, Updike graduated from Harvard College in 1954, and spent a year at the Ruskin School of Drawing and Fine Art in Oxford, England. From 1955 to 1957, he was a member of the staff of *The New Yorker*, to which he has contributed poems, short stories, essays, and book reviews. Since 1957, as a freelance writer, he has lived with his wife in Beverly Farms, Massachusetts, and is now the author of more than fifty books. Among his volumes of poetry are: *Americana and Other Poems*; *Collected Poems 1953-1993*; and *Facing Nature*. His novels and short-story collections include: *Gertrude and Claudius*; *Licks of Love: Short Stories and A Sequel*; and the acclaimed bestseller, *Rabbit, Run*. Updike has received numerous honors and awards including: the National Book Award; American Book Award; National Book Critics Circle Award; and a National Arts Club Medal of Honor. He was awarded a Pulitzer Prize in 1982 for *Rabbit is Rich* and another Pulitzer Prize in 1990 for *Rabbit at Rest*. John Updike's most recent books are: *The Early Stories: 1953-1975* (Ballantine, 2004); a novel, *Villages* (Knopf, 2004); and, to be released in November, *Still Looking* (Knopf, 2005). ✍ **GERARD VAN DER LEUN** is a recovering book and magazine editor and publisher, sometime writer, one-time literary agent, and website publisher (American Digest at www.americandigest.org) on the run from New York City. Currently ensconced with a great wife and wonderful step-son in the hills above the Pacific at Laguna Beach, he's starting the third act in This American Life. ✍ **FRANÇOIS VILLON**, (1431-1463?) born François de Montcorbier in Paris the year Joan of Arc was burned at Rouen, became the greatest writer of 15th-century France, and the first creative, modern French lyric poet. His work is noted for its extraordinary quality, but it is his intensely personal message, rare for its time, that puts Villon in the rank of the moderns. What is known about Villon is gathered from numerous school and police records. In 1452, he earned a Masters from the Sorbonne. In 1455, he got into a fight with a priest and killed him, but was pardoned a few months later on grounds of having acted in self-defense. The ensuing years record a history of arrests, allegations, prisons and pardons, and a life lived among a gang of the student-thieves common in France. It is with this gang that he began writing his ballades in the jargon or *argot* of his fellows. Besides his various chansons, rondeaux, and ballades in jargon, Villon's work consists of *The Legacy* (*Le Lais*, 1456), a series of burlesque bequests to his friends and enemies; and *The Testament* (*Le Testament*, 1461), which follows the same scheme but is far superior in depth of emotion and in poetic value. ✍ **LINA RAMONA VITKAUSKAS** is a Lithuanian-American poet and short fiction writer with an M.A. in Creative Writing from Wright State University. She is the co-editor of the online literary magazine, *milk* (www.milkmag.org), with editor, poet, and critic Larry Sawyer. Vitkauskas' work has appeared in numerous publications, including: *The Prague Literary Review*; *The Chicago Review*; *Yalla* (Montréal); *Bridges* (The Lithuanian-American Journal); and *In Posse Review Multi-Ethnic Anthology* (Ilya Kaminsky, editor). Her most recent chapbook is *Shooting Dead Films with Poets* (Fractal Edge Press, 2004). She lives in Chicago, Illinois. ✍ **PHILLIP WARD**, writer, poet, artist, and photographer, is the editor of Quentin Crisp's forthcoming book, *Dusty Answers*, curator of the Quentin Crisp Archives (www.crisperanto.org)

and executor of his estate. Ward's chapbooks include *Fragmented Images*, *Blue Skies & A Margarita*, and *Winged Flights*. His work has been published in various journals, books, and on the Web. He lives in New York City. ✍ **KAREN WEISER** lives in New York. Her two recent chapbooks are, *Eight Positive Trees* (Pressed Wafer, 2002) and *Placefullness* (Ugly Duckling Presse, 2004). Forthcoming poems can be found in *Jacket* and *Boogcity*. ✍ **C. K. WILLIAMS** was born in 1936 in Newark, New Jersey. He is the author of numerous books of poetry, including: *The Singing* (Farrar, Straus, and Giroux, 2003); *Repair* (1999), which won the 2000 Pulitzer Prize; *The Vigil* (1997); *A Dream of Mind* (1992); *Flesh and Blood* (1987), which won the National Book Critics Circle Award; *Tar* (1983); *With Ignorance* (1997); *I Am the Bitter Name* (1992); and *Lies* (1969). Williams has also published five works of translation: *Selected Poems of Francis Ponge* (1994); *Canvas*, by Adam Zagajewski (with Renata Gorczynski and Benjamin Ivry, 1991); *The Bacchae of Euripides* (1990); *The Lark. The Thrush. The Starling. (Poems from Issa)* (1983); and *Women of Trachis*, by Sophocles (with Gregory Dickerson, 1978). Among his many awards and honors are an American Academy of Arts and Letters Award, a Guggenheim Fellowship, the Lila Wallace-Reader's Digest Award, the PEN/Voelcker Award for Poetry, and a Pushcart Prize. Williams teaches in the creative writing program at Princeton University and lives part of each year in Paris. ✍ **DAISY ZAMORA** won Nicaragua's National Poetry Prize, *Mariano Fiallos Gil*, in 1977. Author of three widely read books of poetry in Spanish, and the editor of the first anthology of Nicaraguan women poets, she also published a book about the concepts of cultural politics during the Sandinista Revolution. A combatant in the National Sandinista Liberation Front, she was the program director and voice of the clandestine Radio Sandino, and became Vice-Minister of Culture after the triumph of the Revolution. Through her life she has been a political activist and advocate for women's rights. Her poems, essays, articles and translations have been published in magazines and literary newspapers throughout Latin America, the Caribbean, the U.S., Canada, Europe, Australia, and Vietnam. Her poems appear in more than forty anthologies in Spanish, English, French, German, Swedish, Italian, Bulgarian, Russian, Vietnamese, Chinese, Dutch, Flemish, Slovak and Czech. English translations of her work include *Clean Slate* (Curbstone, 1993), *Riverbed of Memory* (City Lights, 1992), *Life for Each* (Katabasis, England 1994), and *The Violent Foam* (Curbstone, 2002). She has given poetry readings and lectures throughout the world, including many venues in the U.S., and was a featured artist in Bill Moyer's PBS series *The Language of Life*. In 2002 she was awarded a California Arts Council Fellowship for poetry, and the Nicaraguan Writers Center Literary Acknowledgment for valuable contributions to Nicaraguan Literature. ✍ **HARRIET ZINNES** is a poet and writer whose many books include: *Drawing on the Wall* (poems); *Entropisms* (prose poems); *The Radiant Absurdity of Desire* (short stories); *Ezra Pound and the Visul Arts* (criticism); and *Blood and Feathers* (translations from the poetry of Jacques Prevert). Forthcoming are a collection of poems, *Whither Nonstopping*, and a collection of published literary criticism, *Meaning, Extended*. She is a contributing editor of *The Denver Quarterly* and of *The Hollins Critic* and as art critic contributing writer of *New York Arts Magazine*. She is professor emerita of English of Queens College at the City University of New York.

GALWAY COUNTY LIBRARIES

ACKNOWLEDGMENTS

Maya Angelou: "A Brave and Startling Truth" from *A Brave and Startling Truth* (Random House) by Maya Angelou. Copyright © 1995 by Maya Angelou. Reprinted by permission of the poet.

Ian Ayres: "Kitchen Note to the Masses" first appeared in the online magazine *Exquisite Corpse* (www.exquisitecorpse.org), Cyber Issue 11, Spring/Summer 2002. Copyright © 2002 by Ian Ayres. Reprinted by permission of the poet.

Margaret Atwood: "On Writing Poetry" from the *Margaret Atwood* website (www.owtoad.com) by Margaret Atwood. Copyright © 1995 by Margaret Atwood. Reprinted by permission of the author.

Leonard Cohen: "The Drunkard Becomes Gender-Free" from the *Leonard Cohen* website (www.leonardcohenfiles.com) by Leonard Cohen. Copyright © 1996 by Leonard Cohen. Reprinted by permission of the poet.

James Dean: "Ode to a Tijuana Toilet" courtesy Jonathan Gilmore Collection by James Dean. Copyright © 1955 by James Dean. Reprinted by permission of Jonathan Gilmore.

Brendan Kennelly: "I Can't Say What's Wrong" from *Cromwell* (Bloodaxe Books) by Brendan Kennelly. Copyright © 1988 by Brendan Kennelly. Reprinted by permission of the poet.

Galway Kinnell: "The Dead Shall Be Raised Incorruptible" from *The Book of Nightmares* (Mariner Books) by Galway Kinnell. Copyright © 1973 by Galway Kinnell. Reprinted by permission of the poet.

Nelson Sullivan: "For Sylvia" courtesy Sylvia Miles Collection by Nelson Sullivan. Copyright © 1987 by Nelson Sullivan. Reprinted by permission of Sylvia Miles.

SUBMISSION GUIDELINES

Van Gogh's Ear: Best World Poetry and Prose is an annual anthology series, appearing in January, devoted to publishing excellent poetry and creative writing in English by major voices and innovative new talents from around the globe. Without affiliation with specific movements or schools of poetry/prose, we seek only to publish the best work being written.

If you find our anthology series interesting enough for you to entrust your work to it, we encourage you to subscribe. Our continued existence, and continued ability to read your work, depends mainly on subscriptions and reading fees. We now ask a reading fee of 10 US dollars or 8 euros for submissions from non-subscribers. Checks/money orders in US dollars must be made out to "COP-Van Gogh's Ear". Checks/money orders in euros must be made out to "French Connection Press". Reading fees can also be paid online by credit card (via PayPal) via the Submissions page at the French Connection website (www.frenchcx.com) in US dollars, Canadian dollars, British pounds and euros.

We're open to all styles of poetry and creative writing. Our goal is not to limit anyone in any way whatsoever. We believe that by limiting others, we'd be limiting ourselves. We equally embrace work that shows mastery of versification alongside wild work inspired by Rimbaud's "derangement of all the senses". We not only encourage the exploration of every possible approach to poetry and creative writing, but going beyond anything yet imagined. We are very open to poets and writers who haven't been published before. Being published isn't as important as the work itself.

Submissions should be accompanied by a return address, e-mail address or fax number, and a brief bio of up to 120 words. Name and address of poet/writer should appear on all pages. Copyright automatically reverts back to the author after publication. Submit up to 6 poems or 2 prose pieces at a time. Poem length shouldn't be more than 165 lines and prose length no more than 1,500 words. Previously published work discouraged. No simultaneous submissions. Cover letter preferred; include SAE with IRCs. Time between acceptance and publication is 1 year. Seldom comments on rejections. Published contributors receive one free copy of the volume in which their work appears. Our annual deadline is July 4. Submissions in hard copy (e-mail, fax and disk submissions will not be considered) should be addressed only to: French Connection Press, 12 rue Lamartine, 75009 Paris, France.

To explore much more, please visit us online at: **www.frenchcx.com**

French Connection Press presents *Van Gogh's Ear*, an annual poetry anthology based in Paris and published in conjunction with Allen Ginsberg's Committee on Poetry in New York. Since its début in 2002, *Van Gogh's Ear* has gained international acclaim for its handsome presentation of innovative work by more than eighty celebrated and emerging talents per volume. The *Van Gogh's Ear* series is highly recommended as a rich resource for teachers and a library basic.

Van Gogh's Ear, Volume One is a spirited exploration of poetry characterized by experimentation with form, a revitalized interest in the lyric, and journeys into daring realms of imagination. Among this book's many highlights are Joyce Carol Oates' intense prose poem of sex and murder "Erotic Fantasy in Fast Forward"; Victor Bockris' haunting, prophetic poem "New York City Footsteps"—written just five days before 9/11; Susan Howe's "The Chair", which achieves a rare synthesis of linguistic rigor and humor; "Labor: A company job", the last poem John Wieners ever wrote—included is a letter by him (in his writing) about the poem; plus Rod Smith's "Junkspace Canto", a canto as stingingly accurate as the jab of a needle, with perceptions wound into a jagged sweet music like a gypsy violin.

Van Gogh's Ear, Volume Two, with its cover painting by Vincent van Gogh, offers a knock-out array of fresh, exciting poems— Beat, Slam, Nuyorican, Experimental, you name it—by such daring poets as Peter Orlovsky, Gayle Danley-Dooley, Pedro Pietri, and the list goes on. The result is a dynamic volume chock-full of the verve and artistry of a new millennium of poetry. You'll experience Bob Perelman's "Writing Time With Quotes", showing he can keep more themes and images active simultaneously in a reader's imagination than almost any other poet alive; Paul Auster's "Notes From a Composition Book", a poem that challenges our concepts of what is real and what is word; Dennis Cooper's chilling "A Symphony of Confusion for the People I Killed"; and "The Theorist has No Samba!" by Edwin Torres, selected from this volume for inclusion in *Best American Poetry 2004*.

Van Gogh's Ear, Volume Three is a groundbreaking collection of poems from five continents celebrating the erotic spirit in all of its forms. From the passion of sexual desire to the intense longing for spiritual union, this extraordinary bon voyage turns each page of *Van Gogh's Ear 3* into an exciting discovery. Among the many memorable works included are "And Have You Been Forgotten,", a far-reaching poem by one of the most challenging and engaging radical female poets at work today, Alice Notley; "Holy Drag", by John Rechy, dares peek into the sacristy during changing time for a high Mass presided over by the Cardinal in Rome; "If This is Love" and "Hako" are imaginative, piercing poems by Yoko Ono that appear with two of her intimate *Franklin Summer* drawings. Other impressive drawings, one by Allen Ginsberg, are also included in this landmark anthology.

PLEASE SUBSCRIBE

You can subscribe to the *Van Gogh's Ear: Best World Poetry and Prose* anthology series and become part of a growing network of innovative poets, authors, and readers around the world. Secure online credit card payment is now possible at the French Connection website (www.frenchcx.com); where the purchase of single volumes or subscriptions are available in US dollars, Canadian dollars, British pounds and euros through PayPal, just follow the links.

FOR A SINGLE VOLUME:

$18/14 € (includes postage) per copy of Volume 1
$18/14 € (includes postage) per copy of Volume 2
$18/14 € (includes postage) per copy of Volume 3
$19/15 € (includes postage) per copy of Volume 4

FOR MULTIPLE VOLUMES/SUBSCRIPTION:

$34/26 € for two volumes
(includes postage, please let us know which volumes)

or

$49/38 € for three volumes
(includes postage, please let us know which volumes)

CHECKS ARE WELCOME IN US DOLLARS/EUROS:

Checks are welcome in US dollars payable to: "COP-Van Gogh's Ear" and posted to: Committee on Poetry/Van Gogh's Ear, P.O. Box 582, Stuyvesant Station, New York, NY 10009, U.S.A.

&

Checks are welcome in euros payable to: "French Connection Press" and posted to French Connection Press, 12 rue Lamartine, 75009 Paris, France.

DONATIONS ARE WARMLY APPRECIATED:

Please help keep *Van Gogh's Ear: Best World Poetry and Prose* alive. The continued existence of this groundbreaking anthology series is dependent on subscriptions and donations. All who donate will be acknowledged in upcoming editions and on our website: www.frenchcx.com

Thank you!